How to Plan Your Own

Destination Wedding

HOW TO PLAN YOUR OWN

Destination Wedding

DO-IT-YOURSELF TIPS FROM AN EXPERIENCED PROFESSIONAL

SANDY MALONE

Skyhorse Publishing

Skyhorse Publishing books may be purchased in bulk at special discounts for sales promotion, corporate gifts, fund-raising, or educational purposes. Special editions can also be created to specifications. For details, contact the Special Sales Department, Skyhorse Publishing, 307 West 36th Street, 11th Floor, New York, NY 10018 or info@skyhorsepublishing.com.

Skyhorse® and Skyhorse Publishing® are registered trademarks of Skyhorse Publishing, Inc.®, a Delaware corporation.

Visit our website at www.skyhorsepublishing.com.

10 9 8 7 6 5 4 3 2 1

Library of Congress Cataloging-in-Publication Data is available on file.

Cover design by Jane Sheppard
Cover photo credit: Dollar Photo

ISBN: 978-1-63450-753-0
Ebook ISBN: 978-1-63450-754-7

Printed in China

$\mathcal{C}$ONTENTS

ഇൗരു

$\mathcal{I}$NTRODUCTION

$\mathcal{EOCB}$

$\mathcal{I}$ am an *experienced* professional destination wedding planner, and I'm telling you that without the right tools and guidance, trying to do it yourself (DIY) for your destination wedding is a bad idea. When you DIY, you want to make sure your wedding will go off as flawlessly, and be as much fun for the bride and groom, as it would have if you had paid a professional planner. If you're committed to planning your own wedding thousands of miles away from home, *do it the right way* from the beginning so you get the desired results. You only get one chance to get it right in wedding planning.

I was the original DIY bride. No, really, I was. Twelve years ago, when I was planning my own Caribbean destination wedding, there was no Pinterest, no Instagram, no Wedding Wire, or any other really effective online wedding planning resource or tool available to help me plan a wedding on a tropical island located seven miles off the coast of another Caribbean island. The Knot and the Wedding Channel were in their infancy and mostly just portals for wedding guests to find bridal registries, so I had to do all the research myself. Planning from scratch, for a wedding location where almost everything publicly available was only printed in Spanish, and the Internet was ten years behind the continental United States (which means there wasn't any), was no easy task. Seriously.

Was I daunted? Hell no. I'm a troubleshooter by nature and had spent the last ten years of my life putting out massive political fires for my clients and employers. After all, I had represented the Government of Puerto Rico, the wrong side of the "do not call" lists for telemarketers, and the payday loan industry during my tenure at public relations firms and in representing a big corporation. Tackling something as simple as planning my own destination wedding would be a snap, right? I'd planned press conferences and major corporate and trade events for work, and I'd planned several big-budget weddings in DC for friends, just for fun. I had no fear.

In actuality, I had no idea what I was getting myself into when I undertook the challenge of planning my own destination wedding. There weren't even any decent how-to books to help me with the process. What a nightmare! But when the day finally arrived, my guests thought it was perfect, and in the end, that was what was most important to me. Unfortunately, I was stressed out and didn't have nearly as much fun as my guests. Thus, my goal is to provide other DIY brides and grooms with the tools to make the planning organized enough that you can, in fact, enjoy your own DIY wedding much more than I did.

The success of my own wedding—and the lack of fun I had at the actual events because I was the one running everything—was what eventually inspired my husband and me to move to Vieques Island and open our own Caribbean destination wedding planning company. It wasn't easy, but we did it. You name it, we've got it—or we know how and where to track it down on Vieques or another island nearby. If you can afford it, I can find it. But it took

Sandy and Bill Malone on their wedding day, September 4, 2004, on Vieques Island.

me years to get this all figured out. It's not something I could have DIY'd when I got married. And even though more destination wedding spots can be discovered online today, wedding planning in a remote location is still the biggest DIY challenge any couple could possibly undertake. But you *can* do it (and do it well) if you plan it like a professional would.

Over the more than eight years I've been planning weddings in the Caribbean, I've seen the dramatic shift in the mentality of my brides and grooms, from them wanting me to do everything *for them* to the wedding couples wanting to do everything *themselves*.

Even doing it yourself has taken on a different meaning, though. Five years ago, it was just about hand-making wedding

You can have a devastatingly beautiful ceremony setup with just a few tiki torches, a rose-petal-covered aisle, and an amazing view. (Photo by Morris Malakoff)

favors and creative place cards at home. Now, brides and grooms with the DIY bug want to ship entire centerpieces and boxes of homemade goodies. Never mind the fact that half of what they ship arrives in boxes that look like a fat man sat on them the entire trip, or that half of what they send (if they don't follow instructions) melts en route to the tropics. These couples are determined to create some part of their weddings themselves, if only so they can claim they did it. It's rewarding, because many times I was a part of helping them figure out how to actually make their DIY dreams become a reality. More often than not, my interns and I are the ones doing half the assembly and all the repair work when things arrive.

I gave up trying to steer my brides and grooms away from DIY. There's no point in fighting them. After all, I was the original DIY bride, and I shipped thirty-two boxes of wedding crap to myself via UPS for my own destination wedding in Vieques, Puerto Rico. I even ordered specially-labeled bottled water and had it shipped. What was I thinking? Some brides spend less on their wedding gowns than I did on shipping alone! I hand-painted glass Christmas ornaments for each and every guest as a wedding favor, carefully wrapped them with gorgeous bows, and shipped ALL of it to the Caribbean. We couldn't even walk into our bridal suite at the hotel when we arrived—there were boxes everywhere stacked taller than me! And we spent the better part of the next two days prepping and distributing everything for the guests. That was LOTS of fun and a great way to start our wedding weekend exhausted. But we did it ourselves and lots of other couples want to do it too. This book gives DIYers the opportunity to learn from my mistakes rather than repeat them. I'm not just a wedding planner—I was a DIY bride before it was cool.

Instead of fighting the rising wave of DIYers who wanted to work with me planning their weddings, in recent years I've started helping them do as much of it themselves as they want (and then fixing what they screwed up once it has arrived). Every set of my clients receives a forty-plus-page client guide once they've hired me. Yes, it's the "Do's and Don'ts" and "Thou Shalt Nots"—but really it's chock-full of guidance on how to ship your wedding gown if you choose to do so, why it's a bad idea to mail anything perishable if it can be avoided, and how to mail the things you shouldn't if you really, really want to give it a try anyway.

My goal is for DIY couples, both gay and straight, to plan the same kind of flawless events I plan using the highly-effective system I've created to manage weddings for all of my brides and grooms over the years. I'm going to teach DIY brides and grooms how to do it properly, with none of this half-assed, getting-taken-advantage-of crap that I experienced with my wedding. There's a right way and a wrong way to plan a destination wedding.

It's also important to realize that you *can* hire some professionals for your DIY wedding. Not having a wedding planner means you're a DIY-er. There's absolutely no rule that says you can't hire as many professional vendors as you want to execute your actual festivities.

All DIY couples truly need some guidance from the very beginning so they don't screw everything up, piss off all of the vendors, and end up having to take out a home-equity loan to cover the budget overage that they heaped upon themselves. That is what my book is all about.

CHAPTER 1

༄༅༅

SHOULD YOU HAVE
A DESTINATION WEDDING?

*D*espite an overwhelming desire by some couples to get married on a sandy, sun-drenched beach, or on top of a snow-peaked mountain, sometimes a destination wedding is not practical for any number of reasons. The first thing a bride and groom need to do after they get engaged—but before they start publicly discussing wedding details—is decide between the two of them whether they want to get married in the bride or groom's hometown, in the city where they currently live, or at a destination someplace completely different and new to most of those people who will be invited.

Questions to Ask Yourselves

First, there are practical matters to consider. Can the most important people in your lives all travel, with relative ease, to someplace far away from home? If you have physically disabled VIPs on your guest list, you have to take that into account before you ask them to travel to a destination that is not handicap-friendly. There are plenty of destinations that have all the modern conveniences to make wheelchair accessibility a non-issue. But if your grandmother, to whom you've always been very, very close, cannot travel at all, you must consider whether the day will be as meaningful to you if she cannot be there to share it.

Taking Special Needs into Consideration

If you're going to be accommodating wheelchair-bound or other disabled guests at a destination, you need to choose a well-equipped place like the El Conquistador Resort in Fajardo, Puerto Rico or the Carambola Beach Resort in St. Croix, US Virgin Islands, or something equally modernized in the destination of your choice. You need to ask *lots of questions about accessibility* when you are investigating your destination options. Some of the smaller boutique hotels will only have one handicap-friendly room. Is that enough for your group?

In general, more remote destination wedding locations will present greater challenges for you. Many of the venues that will be suggested for your events will have stairs and no ramp. Good luck finding elevators. I think we have a total of three on all of Vieques. Most bathroom doorways will not accommodate a wheelchair. You have to ask about the facilities and options ahead of time, and if you still want to get married at that destination despite a lack of handicap accommodations at the destination, talk to the specific guest who will be affected.

Considering the Cost to Your Guests

Can the vast majority of your guests afford to attend a destination wedding? Don't assume that everybody has several thousand dollars to drop on a trip to someplace remote for the most important day of *your* life—not everyone will be able to afford the trip and not everyone will have vacation days to burn. You can't pay for everybody's travel and accommodations (and if you can, stop trying to DIY your wedding and hire yourself a "platinum" wedding planner to do all the hard work for you). But assuming that you're only paying for the wedding events you're holding at your destination and not the guests' other expenses, you must accept that some guests won't attend for financial reasons, even if they never tell you that was the reason they aren't coming.

Perks of Having a Destination Wedding

Having considered those two questions, a destination wedding can be the perfect compromise for brides and grooms whose wedding guests are already spread all over the country and, in some cases, the globe. If more than 50 percent of your guest list is going to have to hop a plane to attend your wedding wherever you hold it, having a destination wedding someplace beautiful, fun, and unusual may be the perfect way to make it fair to everyone.

One unintended benefit of a destination wedding is that it allows the brides and grooms to make completely independent wedding decisions without having the pressure of expectations from their parents who live in their hometown. This is good if you're trying to avoid interference, but can be bad if you're breaking their hearts by not getting married in your church at home. Even though I knew *with absolute certainty* that I was getting married on Vieques Island, it was something that remained a struggle for me as well.

My Own Destination Wedding Decision

Even though my mom had visited the destination where I wanted to get married many times and loved it, she had spent the prior thirty years planning out my wedding in her head. That plan involved the

Episcopal church where my brother and I went to school and where I had been an acolyte, followed by a reception at Congressional Country Club near our home in Potomac, Maryland.

We used to play a game we invented called "Plan the Wedding" on long family car trips together when I was very little. No, I didn't grow up wanting to be a wedding planner—I got my degree in journalism and became a reporter in my first professional life. But throughout high school and college, I was always the one who organized the pre-parties and after-parties for dances, much to the chagrin of my Catholic girls' school's headmaster. Growing up, I co-hosted countless bridal showers, baby showers, and engagement parties with my mother for my former babysitters and other special people in our lives. I never realized it, but mom was grooming me for event planning before I started kindergarten.

So even though I had warned my mother several times pre-engagement that I wanted to get married on the tiny island off the coast of Puerto Rico that had been my client more than ten years before, she was still pretty heartbroken that I wasn't going to have the wedding of *our* dreams that we'd planned so many years ago. My fiancé wanted a destination wedding because that's what I wanted, and having been married before, he was willing to let his first-time bride make pretty much all of the decisions.

So Mom and I struck a compromise—a destination wedding weekend in Vieques for fifty guests, with her best friend (my godmother, who also happens, conveniently, to be an Episcopalian priest) officiating, followed by a black-tie reception back in the Washington, DC, area a week later that would include everyone on her "must-invite" list and everyone else we hadn't included for the ceremony on the island. Was it really a compromise? Probably not. At the end of the day, we basically had a destination wedding and a hometown wedding because the reception in DC grew to be so massive. Could we afford all that? Sort of. But I'm going to tell you more about my budget when we get to Chapter 5 and talk about yours.

Breaking the News to Your Parents

The good news is that destination weddings are a hot trend, and your parents may be thrilled with the idea of winging away to a warm spot in the middle of winter back home. Also, destination weddings tend to reduce the overall wedding costs for parents because more destination wedding couples pay for a larger portion of their own weddings, and have smaller guest lists. So, without realizing it, your desire for a smaller wedding someplace remote may actually be a relief if their own professional community obligations would have forced them to get a second mortgage to help fund a hometown bash.

With that said, it's best to discuss the fact that you're *seriously considering* a destination wedding with both sets of your parents as if you do want their input, rather than presenting it is as a fait accompli. Let's face it—most parents want to feel like their opinions count and that you've considered their wishes in making a big decision, like having a destination wedding. Even if you and your fiancé are pretty set in your own minds, try to have an open mind when you sit down and share the good news with your families. It's possible that they will point out some major roadblock to your plan that you hadn't even thought of—but it's just as likely that your mother will start wardrobe planning (at least mentally) once she has visions of palm trees, for example, dancing in her head.

If they oppose your decision completely, don't end the conversation there and then and announce that they have to suck it up because it's your wedding, regardless of how badly you want to fight back. Let them have some time to think about and discuss what you've told them and to do a little research on their own about your destination before you bring it up again. Sometimes fighting an away-from-home wedding is just a natural instinct for parents who have always envisioned something different. Once they realize that a destination wedding doesn't diminish their role in the actual ceremony and reception in any way, they may change their minds completely. To some parents who aren't as familiar with destination weddings, or who have never attended one, they may be hearing "elopement" when you talk about running away to get married. Make it clear from the beginning that you're not eloping. You're running away and inviting everyone you love to come along with you to celebrate the happy day.

Committing to the Decision

Once you and your fiancé are determined to have a destination wedding and have considered all the pros and cons, commit to it. Regardless of their initial reactions, let your parents know that that's going to be the game plan and you'd really like them to get on board. Most of the time, they'll suck it up and go along with it because they don't want to miss being a part of your day and they really do want you to be happy.

If your mom feels like you're getting married elsewhere just to cut her out of the planning process (and it's not true), then involve her in your destination wedding plans early on. You've decided to DIY a wedding someplace you do not live. You're going to need her help. Make sure your parents know that you need and want their input and help (even if you don't follow all of the advice they offer).

CHAPTER 2

ಲಾಞ

CLEANING UP AND FINALIZING
YOUR GUEST LIST

*Y*ou cannot start planning a wedding without an actual invitation list. True, the rate of people who decline is higher with destination weddings, but you still have to have a good idea of how many guests you're going to have to pay for before you can start budgeting and figuring out what you can actually afford.

This is a "reality check" chapter for you DIYers about writing—and then cutting down—your guest list, and it's truly where you have to start this process. The entire experience can be brutal for you as a couple and, most especially, your parents if they really wanted you to have a big wedding at home. But it must be done early so that you and your family can set other people's expectations regarding invitations.

Setting Expectations About Who Will Be Invited

Unless you actually want all three hundred guests that would have been on your hometown list to show up at your destination wedding, you have to make your plans clear when folks who won't be invited are congratulating you on your engagement. People will ask about your wedding plans—it's natural curiosity from people who care about you. Politely telling *everyone* from the outset that you're planning an intimate destination wedding that mostly family is invited to will put them on alert that they might not be invited. If they do receive an invitation to the destination wedding, they'll feel flattered and very loved.

Do not talk about your wedding plans in large groups of people who are not invited. Do not discuss the details on your social media. Bragging about the amazing wedding you're planning to Facebook friends who won't be invited is rude. Nobody likes to have their nose rubbed in the fact that they're not a *good enough* friend to be included as a guest at your wedding. Also, social media news travels far and wide—fast! If you're not inviting all of your extended family and good friends to your destination wedding, you could get into trouble with some people who are very important to you. You might end up having to add them to the invitation list or risk losing the relationship. Be discreet about your wedding plans and, if anything, play them down and avoid discussing them at all in front of people who aren't invited.

If you can't control your mouth, your status updates, and your tweets, the size of your guest list is going to grow, whether you like it or not. If you can afford that, great! If you cannot, try to keep a lid on the details. But don't underestimate how many of your invitees will accept the invitation. I've had some very unhappy brides and grooms who doubled their budgets by inviting too many people at the outset.

Taking the First Whack at Your Invitation List

Painful as it is to tackle, you can't start budgeting and planning until you know how many guests you have, so this is a key launching pad for all those DIYers who think they're ready to start calling venues and booking.

I ask every single potential and new client the same two-pronged question: 1) How many guests do you have on your *actual* invitation list; and 2) How many of them do you guestimate will actually accept the invitation? Some of the answers I get are absolutely hilarious! Even though you can expect fewer guests at a destination wedding, it is not realistic to think you're going to invite two hundred guests and end up with only forty-five actual attendees. If you're running your own numbers like that, you are going to totally screw your budget from the very beginning.

Seriously, one of the most frustrating problems I have as a wedding planner is dealing with hysterical brides who are waaaay over their intended budgets because they had me plan and budget everything for fewer than fifty guests, but when the RSVP cards all came back, they had ninety-five mouths to feed. A wedding that was supposed to be capped at $20,000 can easily creep closer to $40,000 under those circumstances. It's not pretty. The moral of the story is that you have to be realistic about your guest list from the beginning.

Making Tough Decisions

If either or both of you come from big families, the guest list will be a nightmare for you. I know this because I had the same problem. If I had invited all of my aunts and uncles and first cousins (and their spouses) just on my mother's side to my destination wedding, that would have been more than half of the fifty guests invited. Then there were thirteen in our wedding party (including us), plus some spouses. Then there was my dad's side to consider. And if we included them, my fiancé Bill wouldn't even be able to invite his family. It just wasn't going to work. So we had to be brutal. You have to do it the same way.

Getting Started

Open up a fresh Excel spreadsheet and start the list. If you know you'll be having a reception back home later for those who are not invited, go ahead and start a separate page for those names, which will save you time later. Plus, before you're done with this exercise, you will have moved a lot more names over to the reception-only list. Sorry, but that's a fact.

If parity is going to be a problem with regard to which of you has more people on the list, make two separate columns—one for you and one for your fiancé. Or make one list and color-code the names as "yours," "mine," and "ours."

Put your own names at the top of the list—you're part of all of the headcounts for budget, too. You don't get dinner for free because you're the bride and groom.

Then list your parents (and their spouses if they're remarried), your siblings and their spouses (and their kids if you're going to invite children), any step-siblings and their spouses, and your grandparents. Then add your wedding party and their spouses. Check out where your invitation number is now and deduct it from your goal to see how many more you can invite. This is usually when most couples break out a bottle of wine or mix some drinks.

You have to decide if you're inviting your aunts and uncles. And your first cousins. And any other extended family with whom you have been close all of your life. It doesn't have to be the same for you and your fiancé; some families are closer than others. Obviously, they all go on the reception back home list, but how many of them can you really afford to invite to your destination wedding? This is something you should discuss with your parents too, although you're not obligated to do what they tell you to do. Based on the decision you've made about how far out into the family tree your invitations will go, add those names to the list. And their spouses.

Now it's time to input the names of your friends, and their spouses or serious significant others, to the list. And probably your boss and his or her spouse should be invited as well, but whether your employer attends depends entirely on the closeness of your relationship. Mine sent a lovely gift but did not attend. Then add any besties at work who must be invited or you'll never be able to go back to work again after the wedding (but do your best to invite as few work friends as possible, because the more you invite, the more who will be hurt that they weren't invited when everyone chats about your wedding around the water cooler).

Don't Forget Your Parents' Friends

I'd bet money that you're already over the maximum number of guests you'd planned to invite, but you're not finished yet. You absolutely, positively have to let your parents invite their very best friends. If you were getting married at home, they'd invite neighbors whose children's wedding they'd attended and some business associates, too. While they're going to have to adjust expectations for your destination wedding, you have to give them room to invite some of their own support system, especially if your parents are divorced and there's any animosity or anxiety when they're around each other.

Remember, your parents are ridiculously proud of you, and seeing you get married is something they've always looked forward to doing with all their friends watching, too. While most of those friends and associates can be included at something back home if necessary, you must give both sets of your parents a few invitation spots for their friends.

The Brutal Next Step

Once your list is compiled (and I strongly urge you to be as completely thorough as possible in your first swipe at it), it's time to reevaluate every name on the list. Depending on how far over your goal your headcount ends up being, and keeping in mind that not everyone you invite will attend, how many people do you need to cut? Be brutal. It may mean not inviting any cousins. You cannot invite one first cousin without including all the others and their spouses. You and your fiancé may both have to agree not to invite anyone from work except your immediate supervisors, and in some cases, those names can move over to the hometown reception list.

Do not fight about the guest list, with your fiancé or with your parents. If things get heated when you're discussing it, walk away and give everybody some time to think. Then approach it again after a break. Sometimes parents who weren't planning to contribute much financially will change their minds in order to get a specific tier of guests who have been cut put back onto the guest list. If they can afford to do it, that's a great way to solve one problem. But you certainly can't count on it before the offer is extended. Also, keep in mind that you don't know where you're getting married yet or how much you're actually going to spend per person on your guests, so there has to be some flexibility moving forward. You may have to eliminate more names, or you may find out that not everything is as expensive as you had anticipated and some people can be added who you didn't think you could invite.

Try to come up with the most solid and complete list you can before you start looking at venues and destinations. A banquet manager at a hotel, or a caterer for a private venue, cannot give you any sort of price quote without having an idea of how many guests they're dealing with at your wedding.

Should You Invite Children to Your Destination Wedding?

This is probably one of the most important decisions that you have to make from the very beginning. Most wedding couples who don't have children of their own don't want to have a bunch of kids at their wedding, with the exception of close family members. Many destination wedding brides and grooms want to invite their guests to enjoy an "adults-only" weekend free of shrieking and screaming and all the usual noises their friends with children endure at home every day. And lots of guests are happy to leave the kiddos at home for a romantic escape.

However, you must be clear from the very first piece of wedding information you send out to your guests that there are *no children invited* if that's how you want it to be. If you are including children beyond a flower girl and ring bearer (who don't actually count as kids for the purposes of this discussion, because they are in the wedding party), you have to be prepared to include the children of any of your friends or family who want to bring them. You cannot tell one cousin she can bring her children but forbid your fiancé's cousin to bring hers. When she arrives at the destination and sees other children as guests, all hell will break loose. And even if she's classier than that and doesn't make a stink, you've caused irreparable harm to the relationship.

So it's an across-the-board decision you have to make at the outset—kids or no kids? Ultimately the decision is yours, but you have to make your preference clear early so that your guests are able to make alternate childcare arrangements. And you have to stick to your guns. If somebody totally disregards your request and plans to bring little ones, the only obligation you have to the children is to provide their parents with whatever babysitting information you're able to get from the hotel or venue. Since you're planning your own destination wedding someplace where you likely don't know many people, they're taking a huge chance leaving a random person alone with their children. They'd be better off bringing their own babysitter with them, and some will.

If you do decide to include children, remember they are part of the headcount if they're big enough to sit at a dinner table with other guests. Although there will probably be a reduced food and beverage rate for those under the age of ten, it still adds up quickly if you're hosting multiple events. Welcome parties, rehearsal dinners, wedding receptions, and farewell brunches all come with per-person price tags. Even when the numbers are a little lower, they add up quickly.

CHAPTER 3

❧❧❧

CHOOSING YOUR WEDDING DESTINATION AND DATE

Where you do want to get married? Did you start on this destination wedding mission with a particular spot in mind? If not, it's time to start—and finish—your research. Figure out if your guests have passports, because that can really limit your options. Make sure that most of your friends and family are going to be able to afford the airfare and accommodations to the destination you choose—going to the Caribbean is a *lot* cheaper than Europe, for example. Dollars don't go far when they're changed into pounds or euros. And you're not picking up the tab for the whole crew. Knowing the invitees on your guest list well will help you decide where the best destination is for your wedding.

Start out by choosing the climate you want for your wedding. Some people really want a cold-weather environment—perhaps a massive ski lodge with wood-burning fires and a view of the slopes for miles around. Others are pining for turquoise blue waters in the background of their wedding photos and nothing short of a

Amy and John knew they wanted to get married on Vieques with their families because they'd visited the island several times and loved it. For them, the decision was easy—no thinking required. (Photos by Colby T. Antonacci)

tropical beach will do. Not everybody needs to leave the continental United States for a destination beach wedding—we have coasts on three sides of this country and there are many, many beautiful beaches available on which to say "I do." Once you've decided on the climate, it will help determine the time of year and location options.

Factors to Consider in Choosing Your Destination

As I mentioned before, if the vast majority of your guests don't have passports, you should be thinking about getting married in North America, Puerto Rico, or the US Virgin Islands. Anywhere else and they're going to need a passport to get there. And for some really lazy people, that's just enough reason to claim they can't come.

Whether you want all of your guests to have to fly to your wedding is also a consideration—not only for them, but for your DIY budget as well. If you can find a mountaintop or beach destination you love within a day's driving distance from your home, you'll save yourselves a fortune by renting a truck or trailer to haul all your DIY wedding décor, favors, and other various items that must get to your wedding destination with you, rather than spending lots of money on shipping costs.

If air travel and shipping aren't considerations and you're determined to get married someplace that requires a flight (if only to escape winter's chill), evaluate the realistic tropical destinations you have as options. I'm constantly surprised by the number of clients from the West Coast who want to get married in the Caribbean. Almost all of them tell me it's because Hawaii's wedding venues are much more expensive and the airfare to get there is usually a lot higher than flights to Puerto Rico. Some say it's because Caribbean beaches are better—white sand versus a lot of volcanic rock—but it's really all a matter of personal preference. Do you two have someplace exotic that is special to you both? Did you spend your first vacation alone together at a special spot in the Florida Keys? Maybe it's time to share your secret destination with the rest of your friends.

Researching Your Destination Options

One thing is certain: Unless your father is Daddy Warbucks, you can't go visit every destination that you're considering for your wedding. You have to really narrow down the list until you've found one place that you think is "the one." If you've never been there, I strongly urge you to visit and spend several days there without anyone knowing you're planning a wedding before you start interrogating banquet managers and caterers. Make sure this is really the place you want to get married. Secretly shop the destination, so to speak. If you're considering several different hotels in one ski area, have lunch or dinner at each of them and check out the quality of the food, the condition of the venue, and the service by the staff. Follow the same plan in a beach town or on an island. Sometimes, locations that look beautiful in other brides' wedding photos may not turn out to be your actual paradise.

Don't rely entirely on a destination's website to tell you about the locale. Do deeper research than that. TripAdvisor.com is a great resource, but there are also a million websites about weddings other couples have had in the destination you're considering. Even if you're not hiring a wedding planner, sites like WeddingWire.com and OneWed.com will help you find vendors for that destination. Moreover, you can surf wedding planners' sites for testimonials by other brides about the destination. If they rave about their fabulous planner but call the island a total shithole, you might want to reconsider your location. There are places that only have one safe and beautiful hotel, and where it's not safe to leave the resort's compound on your own. Is that really where you mean to invite your loved ones to visit? Do your homework. You might not easily find crime stats for areas outside the continental United States, but you can certainly read about other visitors' experiences in the place where you think you want to celebrate your most important day.

Once You Think You've Chosen Your Venue

It's time to share the exciting news with your family and best friends who will definitely be in the wedding party and make sure nobody raises a big red flag when they hear your plan. If they're already prepared for the concept of the destination wedding, they'll likely just be relieved to hear you've made a selection so you can start the planning. But parents aren't stupid, and they often make excellent points. I've planned more than one wedding for couples who had initially planned to get married in Mexico until their parents printed out all the State Department-issued travel warnings about numerous areas in that country where it isn't safe for Americans to travel. Even though they hadn't planned on getting married in that particular Mexican town, learning that a large number of visitors are kidnapped and robbed every year within an hour of where they did want to get married made them change their minds. You want your guests to be excited to tour the destination you choose, not terrified to leave the hotel property.

Nailing Down Your Wedding Date

I recommend that you have two or three dates in mind before you move ahead to look for your wedding venue. Sure, you have a first choice. But what if the venue you're in love with at your destination is already booked that weekend? You should have a second choice ready to go (and a third if you're absolutely, positively certain that is where you want to get married). There's no point in starting the venue research and calling a bunch of properties and villa brokers if you don't know when you're getting married.

Rates change depending on the wedding date. The time of year and day of the week can factor in as well. It's obviously more expensive to get married on a snowy mountaintop during ski season than in the other seasons when local hotels are only half occupied. Similarly, the airfare alone may kill you and your guests headed to some tropical destinations between January and April.

I'm not telling you that you shouldn't DIY your wedding someplace during "high season." Rather, I'm telling you to make an educated decision about the destination that you choose. If airfare and accommodation are two or three times more expensive during a few months of the year, be sure you're aware of that before you sign a contract to get married during that time window.

There's no such thing as doing too much homework. Having a firm grasp on your destination, budget, and head count is what will make it possible for you to move forward with the next wedding planning steps.

CHAPTER 4

ഇൻ‌ൽ

CHOOSING YOUR WEDDING VENUE ONCE YOU KNOW WHERE YOU'RE GETTING MARRIED

*Y*ou've figured out the destination where you're getting married, but now you need to decide *exactly where* at that destination is the best place to have your wedding ceremony, wedding reception, and to accommodate your (sometimes picky) guests. And you have to provide a variety of price-point options in most cases, because not all of your friends can afford to stay at an expensive hotel, even if that's where you're lucky enough to be celebrating your wedding events. Many guests turn destination weddings into their own vacations—justifiably, since they're likely burning some of their precious work leave to be there. You can *suggest* where they should stay, but you cannot force them all to stay at the same place, regardless of how big a pain in the ass that is for you as the DIY bride and groom.

There are lots of different things to consider when choosing your venue—from the size to the cost, the menu options and the bar rates, and what's included versus what you have to bring in

This bride and groom wanted a Caribbean view that wasn't on the beach, and it doesn't get much more beautiful than this ceremony venue at the Blue Horizon Boutique Resort on Vieques. (Photo by Morris Malakoff)

yourself. In many cases, if you're renting a villa or private estate, all you're getting is the house (and permission to have your wedding there). You have to track down everything else, from tables to music. Using a hotel venue limits your options, but can reduce your stress. But lots of DIYers are planning their own destination wedding because they do want to choose each little thing themselves and make it "different" from anything anybody else has had at weddings they've attended. So the bulk of the DIY crew inevitably chooses the harder road (which also happens to be the more traveled one) and rent private properties.

Preparing for a Venue Selection Trip

Buzzkill Alert: Just because you go to your destination to look at venues doesn't mean you're actually going to get to tour every place you're considering for your wedding, especially if you schedule your wedding planning trip during a high-season time at the destination, when the vast majority of the best venues are occupied with other renters. You cannot go traipsing through a privately rented villa while other guests who spent thousands of dollars to rent it are sitting on the pool deck sipping margaritas. The only venues you'll be able to tour are the hotels and any private venue that doesn't have guests. And you must make contact with rental agents ahead of time and then confirm the week of your trip, because if the property got rented in between, you may not be able to visit it after all.

Managing Your Own Expectations

Destination wedding locations and venues aren't the same as wedding venues at home. If you were getting married back in your hometown or another major city, you'd expect to be able to do cake tastings to choose your pastry chef and a menu-selection tasting with your caterer before signing that final contract. This is not the case in more remote locales. When the best pastry chef around runs things from her home kitchen, she probably doesn't do tasting appointments. And if you can finagle one, you're going to have to pay for a privilege that would have probably been free someplace more traditional.

How to Get the Most Out of a Venue Selection Trip

If your first-choice venue is a hotel with a restaurant, taste the food *before* you sign a contract to make that your venue. And I don't mean you demand a free tasting menu. Make a reservation and secretly shop the place. Even if you have an appointment with their in-house event coordinator the very next day to discuss availability and pricing, it's well worth the effort and money spent to experience it as a regular guest to see how good the service is and what you think of the food. If they know who you are when you walk in the restaurant, you might not be getting what your friends will be getting when they decide to have lunch there.

Make appointments *ahead of time* with all of the venues (hotels or private villas) that you want to see. As I've warned you, in the high season you probably won't be able to tour every villa you like because they're occupied, but try. With that said, if you wait until you get to the destination and expect to call on the second day of your trip and be able to successfully achieve all the meetings you need to have with vendors while you're there, you are woefully wrong about what is going to happen. Additionally, chances are your visit will wrap a weekend, and all of the best wedding vendors will probably be busy and in the middle of weddings.

When we get a call on a Friday from a couple who informs me they're getting married here and they're on the island right now, and they want to meet with me before they leave on Monday, I just laugh at them. I'm already booked. And if they are the type of people who expect the whole world to spin around them while they're engaged, I probably don't want to work with them as clients anyway. Caterers, music suppliers, florists, pastry chefs, and a host of other wedding vendors all feel the same way—trust me. You want a practice hair session with the stylist the venue recommends? You need to schedule that in advance. I suggest you book your trip on a weekday and give all of the vendors you want to meet with lots of warning about when you will be there, so you can actually get through at least half of your list. If you don't have appointments with vendors before you go, you're probably not going to meet with them during your trip. And even if you do have an appointment, be sure to confirm it the week before your trip and, again, a day before the actual appointment. We've all experienced the visiting "no-show" client too many times so that ultimately, not everybody takes you seriously. It's really critical to make sure they know you're actually coming and are prepared to meet with you at the appointed time. It will head off a lot of frustration for you.

Choosing the Best Venue for Your Wedding

Do you want to stay together with all your guests under the same roof so you can maximize your time with them? Or do you want to stay apart from most of the crew so you can avoid anxiety attacks when you need some alone time in the days leading up to your wedding? Only you know what suits you best, and you should go to your destination to find it.

Larger Hotel Chains

When you choose to get married at a hotel that is part of a well-known hotel chain, you can have relative certainty that the corporation has certain standards for events like your wedding. With that said, you can't assume that a brand-name hotel in a remote destination is the same as the one by the same name that you visited in New York or Miami. It simply will not be comparable. It might be better in some ways, but there will be other services you'd normally expect from the chain that aren't actually ever available at that particular location. Dry-cleaning and laundry services are one excellent example. Plan to bring your hand-held steamer with you.

Larger hotels will have plenty of rooms for all of your guests to stay together, and they'll usually arrange a discounted rate for your room block—although you'll be committed to filling a certain number of rooms with guests. Beware! If your friends use their own hotel points or book their room through Hotels.com or another online discount broker, their rooms won't count towards filling the rooms you've committed to, so it's often better to reserve fewer rooms unless you have reason to believe they'll be over-booked (on Valentine's Day weekend, for example, you need to hold plenty of space for your guests). But make certain you have a very clear understanding of the room block policy.

Find out if you can release the unclaimed rooms by a certain date if you end up having fewer guests than anticipated. If you can't release the rooms, what's the financial penalty for you and your fiancé? Find out how your guests access the room block—does the hotel provide a personalized web portal for your wedding guests to book, or do they need a specific code to use online? Can they book on the phone, or *must* they book online to take advantage of the wedding group discount? You are your own wedding planner and you have to be prepared to answer all of these questions for your guests.

When you get pricing for your wedding events, find out what they're charging you for each space you're using in addition to the actual food and beverage charges. Find out what the service charges are and if there are additional gratuities on top of that. I've found that most of the bigger hotels have what amounts to about a 30 percent mark-up for service fees, before taxes. Also, find out about the hotel/tourism taxes that will be tacked on to the bottom of your final bill. If you're not in the States, it could be surprising how high those rates are depending on the destination you've chosen. All hotels use some form of "BEO," a banquet event order, to organize your event. You need to see and understand how that paperwork works where you're getting married. It's one thing to leave there thinking you're going to spend $150 per guest for dinner without realizing that you're going to have an additional $5,000 charged for using the space and lighting it up. Just because a hotel offers to have your reception at night on a waterfront lawn doesn't mean they're going to provide the lighting for the event, or let you use the space for free. And obviously, you can't eat in the total dark. Find out all possible additional charges from the beginning.

All-Inclusive Resorts

Many brides and grooms are drawn to the "all-inclusive" concept, thinking that means their guests will save a lot of money attending their wedding. False.

What "all-inclusive" means for your wedding guests is that they're actually pre-paying for all of their meals and drinks—including your wedding events—and they don't get to choose what they actually want to eat and drink part of the time. No, seriously, think about it. The resort will require your guests to fill X number of rooms for X number of days as a part of the package you choose. Then they will charge you for the wedding package that you've chosen on top of that. It's fair that the hotel is charging for your wedding, but it sucks that your guests are basically paying for their own cocktails at your reception.

Most all-inclusive resort packages are very limited. By limited, I mean that the bride and groom get to choose cake A, cake B, or cake C. The bride may choose Bouquet Number 1 or Bouquet Number 2, with room for color preference. The reception menu you'll be choosing from will be fairly generic as well. And, unless you have it in writing from the resort, expect to be one of multiple brides traipsing down the same aisle on the same day at the same venue. You also probably will be re-using some (if not all) of the same décor.

For some couples, that's just fine. They chose a destination wedding because they didn't want to deal with all the little minutiae of the wedding details, and getting married at an all-inclusive resort will certainly help eliminate that. It's probably the easiest

DIY out there, as many resorts even offer your guests "discounted" travel packages to go with their hotel stays. But if you're DIYing your wedding because you want it to be personalized and different, choosing an all-inclusive resort, where you're the third bride getting married with the same wedding décor as the first two on the same day, might not really be what you've had in mind.

Although the budget numbers the resort provides you may be appealing at first, you have to think through the process that got you to that number. You're supposed to be hosting this event, not organizing a reunion where everybody pays their own way. The simple, tacky truth about all-inclusive wedding packages at resorts is that you're asking your guests to spend a lot of money on a trip that results in booking a lot of rooms at the resort so that you get certain pricing on your wedding. Your guests actually help defray the cost of your wedding festivities. When the salesperson at the resort tells you they'll throw in a free welcome cocktail party or a special farewell breakfast the morning after, you're not actually getting anything for free. Your guests have already paid for their food and beverages. The only thing the free event will do is give you a private space while limiting your guests' choices in a resort that probably has a lot of different dining options. That said, it's a great way to get somebody else to pay for your wedding.

Boutique Hotels and Guest Houses

There are many beautiful boutique hotels, historic inns, bed and breakfasts, and other such guest houses with facilities for holding weddings. Usually, you're required to fill all the rooms at the hotel in order to have your event there, because it is the sort of intimate setting where outsiders staying in the midst of your wedding would feel very uncomfortable.

Committing to fill an entire hotel may sound daunting, but it's not difficult if there are a small number of rooms. There are plenty of lovely venues with fewer than twenty rooms on the property. That likely means that fewer than fifty people can actually stay there, depending on the room configurations and their policies about extras in rooms.

Find out whether you have to use the property's on-site restaurant for all of your catering, or if you can bring in somebody from the outside. Find out if they have a list of "preferred" vendors and if there are any vendors they require you to use or whom they prohibit from working on their property. If you really like the venue, you can probably work with them on all those restrictions and end up very happy. However, if you're in love with somebody else's food at a guest house with a restaurant, you might consider renting a private villa for your actual wedding and simply recommending that your friends stay at the other property you were considering.

It's important to understand the maximum number of attendees the venue can hold and make sure there's no way you're going to exceed that. Don't play the numbers too close or you could end up with a real problem. It's not just about paying for the extra heads; rather, it's about whether the reception space can reasonably fit another ten-top dinner table and still leave enough room for the servers to bring food and drinks to your guests.

If you're taking over the entire property, make sure any public entities contained within it (like a bar or restaurant) will be closed to the general public on the day of your actual wedding. You don't want strangers wandering around the periphery of your reception—it's likely that part of the appeal of the property was the privacy you'd have with only your friends and family staying there. Understand ahead of time how the property handles event weekends with the general public.

Private Homes and Villa Rentals

In almost every destination, you will find incredible private homes available to rent for your wedding festivities. Some of these houses will have been used for events many times and it's old hat to the owners and property managers. However, not every owner who rents his villa intends for large parties to be held there. Your first question when investigating a particular house is to ask whether they permit weddings. If the answer is no, don't waste another minute of your time.

Many private rentals charge an "event fee" to pay for the extra wear and tear and maintenance associated with a large event. Sometimes that can be negotiated by a reputable wedding planner, but if you're a DIY couple, don't expect much leniency. The fact of the matter is that they don't know you, and they have no idea what condition you're going to leave a house in the day after your wedding. You'll also be paying a security deposit (sometimes higher than usual when it's for a wedding), and the house managers will be counting *everything* the day after your wedding. If a bunch of drunk guests jump in the pool and then leave the reception wrapped in beach towels your mother kindly handed them, you are going to be billed for each and every missing towel. And don't stuff more guests into the house than the lease allows or you'll likely be billed for that as well. Property managers aren't stupid and the neighbors can count.

The good news is that you probably have the most options with regard to choosing your vendors for a venue that is a private home. The bad news, as a DIYer, is that you're going to have to do significantly more homework on the vendors you choose, because you're starting from scratch. And you may not have anybody on the receiving end to ship things to ahead of time if you're simply renting a house through an agent.

Check out a house carefully if you're able to tour it. Villas, chalets, and other private homes don't come with a front desk and maintenance crew. If the house isn't in good shape, don't expect repairs to be made to anything unless expressly stated in the actual lease.

Booking Newly Constructed Venues

Don't book anything that is still under construction, or even in the middle of a massive renovation. I learned that the hard way my first couple of years in business in the Caribbean. "Island time" is more than just an expression; it's a reality. Not only have we had to move entire weddings a month prior to the big day because houses weren't finished, but I actually had to move two weddings that were booked at a major hotel, because it didn't open on time. Despite being part of a major chain, the hotel finally completed renovations and launched two years after its initially planned opening date.

Worst-case scenario for the property that's not ready is that they have to refund your money. But for you, as a DIY bride and groom, this nightmare can leave you a month out from your wedding with no place to host the event. That is a complete wedding disaster and even if you fix everything at a great new venue, you'll still be a total wreck by your wedding day. No fun at all.

When You Can't Actually Visit Your Destination to Choose Your Venue

I strongly urge DIY destination wedding couples to spend the time and money to visit the spot they've chosen for the most important day of their lives. Sometimes, what looks perfect in pictures online isn't exactly as it appears. It's okay to change your mind after you visit. If you didn't love it, don't get married there. You lost the money for the scouting trip, but at least you're not pouring thousands of dollars into a decision you'll regret for years. I once had a set of clients who had never been to Vieques change their minds when they finally visited the island. Turns out, the bride absolutely hates chickens. If you've been to the Caribbean, you can see why that would have been a challenge, since she wanted me to promise we'd plan her wedding so she would never see a chicken during her whole trip. Can't be done. Better they get married someplace else.

"Rustic cabins" sound very cozy in advertisements, but you want to find out exactly *how* rustic they are. Are you trying to take your family camping, or have an elegant wedding in the woods? Sometimes you're better off letting guests choose from nearby motels and B&Bs than you are forcing them to stay in random cabins. One girlfriend of mine got bedbugs at just such a "rustic" New England property when she attended her sister's wedding. Those aren't the kind of memories you want to give your guests. The entire property was infested.

A very private ski chalet with "breathtaking views" may be located at the top of a treacherous driveway. That's fine if you're getting married on a mountaintop in the States in July, but not in December. How are you going to transport your guests? Discuss and understand the plan with the property managers until it makes sense to you before you sign the lease.

Regardless of how "green" and "eco-friendly" you want your wedding to be, do not assume that all of your guests feel the same way you do about sleeping with no screens in the windows, or not having air-conditioning someplace tropical in the summertime. Yurts and teepees and tree houses sound really cool, but are they practical for your average guest? What looks posh in a professionally staged picture might not live up to expectations in person.

I used those examples because that's how detailed you need to be in your decision-making process. And if you don't go look at the venues you're considering, how can you actually know what you're really getting before you get there? If you absolutely can't go see it ahead of time, do more homework and find some brides and grooms who have websites that say they got married there. Reach out to them directly and ask to talk to them on the phone about their experience with the property.

CHAPTER 5

ಬಂಡ

HOW TO DECIDE ON AND STICK TO A REAL WEDDING BUDGET

*W*ho is paying for your wedding? That's my first question. If it's just you guys, that's easy. But if Mom and Dad (for either of you) are helping, you have to get the exact amount of their contribution up front so you know how much you're working with. Oftentimes, well-intentioned parents suggest they're going to help but don't really come through with as much support as you'd hoped in the end. The economy has made it harder on everybody.

Learn from My Mistake

When I got married, my father said he'd match whatever my mom contributed to our wedding budget. Now keep in mind, I was having a wedding in Puerto Rico for fifty guests, and another three hundred guests for a black-tie affair back in Washington, DC, a week later. We were spending a fortune, and Bill and I intended to pay for most of it ourselves from the beginning (thank God for those stock options I could exercise at my company—they'd seemed so useless a part of my signing bonus). But when we chose a date and started making plans, Dad laid down the law.

"I'll match whatever your mother gives you," he offered. Did I mention they were not-so-amicably divorced not that many years before my wedding? Anyway, my mother and I both took my father at his word, and she gave me a budget, and we started planning with all the money thrown into one pot. It actually worked out quite well until my father found out how much my mother planned to contribute. He was outraged.

Now, I understand that he was comparing the cost of my wedding to my older sister's wedding reception—which was basically a dessert-only, church-basement affair in Ohio (her choice)—but that wedding was also ten years before mine. Plus, my soon-to-be husband was a high-ranking police official and I worked in public affairs in the nation's capital—the guest list of "must-invites" for the hometown reception was not short, especially when you included the one hundred and forty-five "must-invites" my mother insisted were somehow related to me (oh yes, she had that list in an Excel spreadsheet for me within forty-eight hours of Bill's marriage proposal. Methinks she'd been planning ahead for years).

Short story long, Dad did not contribute even close to what my mother chipped in, and Bill and I paid more than either of them (and Mom was *very* generous, don't misunderstand). But our whole plan went in the shitter when my father didn't live up to his end of the budget bargain. Unfortunately, there was no drop-back-and-punt option at that point, because we had booked our wedding venues on both Vieques Island and in Washington, DC, and ordered the invitations for both sets of guests, all before the actual budget imploded on us.

The purpose of this story isn't to make my dad look like a bad guy—he wasn't. He bailed my butt out of a stupid credit card mistake in my twenties and was a pretty generous guy. But my sister royally screwed me with her bargain-basement DIY wedding (long before DIY was even a common expression). Nothing about anything from her wedding could have been compared to mine, so it wasn't fair to compare the budget either.

I shared this story with you because I think it's *really, really important* to talk budget and get specific financial commitments from your parents before you start spending imaginary money. It happened to me, and it can happen to you. In the best possible scenario, your parents will simply give you a check for what they're willing to contribute and let you manage the funds from there. If they're not able to help, at least you'll know it from the beginning.

This is a serious conversation that must be had, first between the bride and groom, figuring out what you can each realistically spend towards your wedding. Count in the credit cards you're planning to use and whatever else; just write down real numbers. Then, when you talk with your parents, you can tell them (or not) how much the two of you are contributing if they feel you're asking for too much help. It would not be considered unreasonable, for example, to ask each set of parents to contribute $5,000 (if they're able) if you guys are putting your own $10,000 in the pot to start. You can have a lot of DIY wedding for $20,000 if you play your cards right.

Sometimes parents want to pay for things more traditionally— etiquette calls for the groom's family to pay for the bride's bouquet, the wedding rehearsal dinner, and the reception bar, among other things. Emily Post gives the privilege of the rest of the tab to the bride's parents. Today, it's not uncommon for the groom's parents to want to pay for a rehearsal dinner in its entirety, keeping with that tradition alone. What you have to figure out is how much a rehearsal dinner is actually going to cost at your destination.

Are you going to have something formal and sit-down, or would you rather have a clam bake or pig roast beach party followed by a fire pit? If the bride and groom have solid opinions on what they want—and those opinions don't necessarily match that of his parents—then it's important to set a contribution amount and leave it at that. Don't let his mom think she's going to be tormenting your caterers at your destination if you're not going to let her have that kind of control.

How to Create Your Budget Spreadsheet

Embarrassing as it is, you have to talk real dollars and cents. Literally. Then create a spreadsheet that starts with your target budget right on top. Start with a column titled "Wedding Expenditures" and then, to the right of that, create the following columns: Estimated Cost, Actual Cost, Deposit Due Date, Deposit Paid Date, Balance Due Date, Balance Paid Date, and Details about Payment Required. Take note from the very beginning about which vendors only accept checks or only take credit cards, and which cards they actually accept. The more remote your destination, the less likely the vendors are to accept anything other than Visa or MasterCard, if they take credit cards at all. It doesn't do you any good to plan a budget around a credit card when the vendors require a cashier's check as payment.

You'll be able to start filling in "Actual Cost" numbers on the spreadsheet for everything as soon as you book your venue and start hiring your vendors. You should plug in your estimates/guestimates at the start and leave as few question marks in the blanks as possible. Write down each and every vendor you think you may be hiring (and add to the list as you hire others), but don't forget to include items you may not think of as vendors, such as the cost of all the favors, décor, and anything else you will be paying for the craft supplies to DIY. And then there will always be gratuities.

Look at the total budget guestimate you come up with after researching and choosing your destination before you start putting down deposits and signing contracts. Don't order invitations until you have real estimates on the per-person costs you're about to incur. And, as I have always preached, don't tell anybody outside the immediate family about the little details of your wedding plans until you've made sure it all fits your budget. Once you've set expectations, it's very hard to go backward. If you end up with a higher acceptance rate than you anticipated, and your catering bill is going through the roof, you might decide you don't really need to put a bottle of booze in each welcome gift, or you might choose to do a simple cake rather than the elaborate dessert buffet you told everybody about. By keeping your detailed plans to yourself, you don't have to save face if something doesn't happen. If you run the numbers and you can't afford your game plan, it's time to start over.

Involving Your Parents in the Budget and the Planning

How much money your parents are contributing to your wedding budget may play into how much involvement you give them in the planning process. You must also consider how much time they're contributing. If you're going to need their actual help the weekend of the wedding because you're DIYing and don't have a wedding planner, tread very lightly here. You can't refuse to let your mother at least show you the pictures of flowers she's taught herself to "Pin" online if you need her to help you with the flowers and assemble the bouquets once you get to your destination. With a wedding planner, it's easy for brides and grooms to tell their parents they can't participate in the planning and blame it on the consultant (even if it's not true), but you cannot and should not do that when you're planning to execute everything yourself on your wedding day. You will need their help. You will need everybody's help.

That said, knowing how much financial help you're getting is key, and when you get a firm commitment of how much you can count on and when you'll actually receive it, put it on a spreadsheet with all the other money you have to work with and start from there. Be sure to ask if they'll be writing you a check and when—they may plan to pick up a tab with a credit card, not realizing how tricky that can be for you with some of the things you're cobbling together at your destination. Promising you $5,000 that can only be accessed on their American Express or Discover card might not actually cut it when it comes time to pay most vendors someplace that almost everybody only takes MasterCard and Visa.

CHAPTER 6

ඊ∽ඌ

NEGOTIATING THE VENUE CONTRACT WITH A PRIVATE OWNER OR HOTEL

Once you've nailed down your destination and your budget, it's time to make a decision and sign a contract for your venue. If you've found your first-choice venue doesn't suit your actual budget, you may need to consider a less expensive option.

If you're getting married at a hotel, they'll have a pretty standard contract for you to read and sign. That's where all the little details I mentioned in the last chapter about event fees, service charges, and gratuities come into play.

As the bride and groom, you basically want to see as few restrictions and assignments of liability as possible. You want to know how many people you can have at the venue, how late your event can run, how many people can stay there, and what services the venue is providing. This should *all* be in writing. Just because the villa's website says it provides maid service doesn't mean that's included in the lease for your wedding weekend. Make sure all the amenities they offered online or when you were touring the property are outlined specifically in the lease.

You have to do the exact same thing with a major hotel chain. If the salesperson with whom you initially spoke about their venue at your destination told you that they would "comp" the bride and groom's room on the wedding night, you should see that in the estimate or proposal they provide you when you're considering the contract. You cannot expect that anything that isn't on the contract will end up being honored by the hotel. Frequently, with large hotels, you are actually working with a corporate event salesperson based someplace entirely different from the hotel. Sometimes the salesperson has never even been to the venue at your destination. Once your contract is signed, they'll pass you off to the event coordinator at your destination and you'll never interact with them again. The person on-site at your destination hotel may not know anything about what verbal promises were made in initial conversations with the salesperson, so you have to get really detailed. Even when you're dealing with somebody at the hotel, a verbal commitment is still no guarantee. Turnover is huge at many resort hotels, and you don't know who you'll be working with eight months down the road when you actually get married. Verbal promises made during a tour, when they're trying to convince you to sign a contract and put down a deposit, don't mean squat when the chips are down and you get a final invoice charging you for the ceremony space they had told you would be free of charge.

Many hotels, including the smaller guesthouses, will give room discounts based on a minimum number of nights to all of your guests. That's something else you need to have in writing. Don't expect to have a lot of negotiating room or buying power if you're getting married someplace popular during their high season, because that just won't happen. If they can fill up the rooms anyway with regular guests, many of whom will stay significantly longer than wedding guests, who are usually there a maximum of three days, they'd rather have those guests instead of your wedding. Don't choose a destination wedding "hot spot" mentioned in every magazine and expect to have bargaining power. That's unrealistic.

Make sure you understand the cancellation policies for yourselves (I'm not implying that you're going to split up—but medical emergencies and deaths in families do occur and can result in changes of plans). Understanding how much you stand to lose can help you decide if you need to invest in wedding insurance, something that has become more popular as the number of destination weddings has dramatically increased. Brides and grooms worry less about dealing with their local florist and country club than an unknown quantity someplace they don't live.

If you're renting a private house or villa, understand their policy if they cancel on you. It really can happen, especially in tourist vacation spots where so many houses are on the market all the time and sell very slowly. If a house that's been for sale for years suddenly sells and the new buyers don't want to honor your rental, how will the current property owner compensate you? It's okay to ask if the house is on the market. That's something else you have every right to know and should consider as part of your educated decision-making process. It doesn't necessarily mean you should not rent that property, but you need to know how the owner plans to handle things if for some reason he cannot fulfill his end of his agreement with you.

Do You Need to Buy Wedding Insurance?
A few years ago, I would have told you that you should buy wedding insurance only if you're the kind of person who always buys travel insurance. But the wedding insurance market has grown, more insurance companies are providing it, and some of the benefits are excellent.

Research the insurance product thoroughly to make sure you are clear on what it does and does not cover, and what you'd need to do to prove a vendor didn't provide satisfactory services in order to recoup your money. Know up front that wedding insurance never covers weddings that are cancelled because a couple splits up, but you don't need to worry about that, right?

Getting a Second Opinion

Even if you're DIYing your wedding, you should still be open to taking advantage of good free advice from close friends and family who know more about some of this than you do. If you've never signed a hotel event contract but you have a girlfriend who works in banquet management at a hotel, ask for her help! Have you ever leased a vacation house? Maybe not; it depends on how old you are when you're getting married. But odds are that your parents have some experience with paperwork like this. Heck, between the two of you, your families, and your best friends, you probably have an attorney somewhere in the bunch. Don't be afraid to ask for help.

Do you know anybody who spends a lot of time at the destination you've chosen? If your parents have friends with a condo in Aspen near the venue you're considering, reach out to them for opinions. If you know somebody who has attended a wedding on a particular island you've fallen in love with, ask her all about it (even though you know that you're not going to have some of the problems the other bride did because you're reading this book first, and you're more organized). Consider it intelligence-gathering and suck up all the information that you can.

Follow your gut instincts. Even if you are married to (pun intended) the idea of having your wedding at a particular villa on a specific island, if something makes you feel hinky during the venue acquisition process, take a moment to back up and reassess the situation. It might be nothing . . . or it might be a reason the venue isn't as perfect as you initially thought it was.

The good news is that now you've tackled some of the hardest parts of wedding planning—you have a guest list, a budget, a destination, and a venue. On to the fun stuff!

CHAPTER 7

 ෨ ೮

WEDDING INVITATIONS—HOW DOES THE WHOLE PROCESS WORK FOR A DESTINATION WEDDING AND WHAT'S THE "WEDIQUETTE"— A MULTI-STEP PROCESS

*Y*ou can't send the invitations until that venue contract is signed, but you can be shopping for them and ready to start ordering as soon as the ink dries on your venue contract. Good invitations take six to eight weeks to print if you don't want to pay rush charges, so start looking right away.

The rules for destination wedding invitations are not the same as anything in traditional weddings. Invites can go in the mail one year prior to the wedding date and still provide your guests the traditional six to eight weeks to reply when they receive it. Be sure to put the RSVP deadline on the invitation, or your guests may not understand its immediacy. But you don't want to mail your guests invitations to a place they know nothing about without first providing them with some information about what's going on and where they need to stay and how much all of this is going to cost them. They won't want to send back an RSVP without having answers to all of these questions.

Whether you send a stand-alone save-the-date or just combine it with the much more important Travel Information Packet is entirely up to you, but you need to get those details together as quickly as possible to share with your guests. Wedding websites are not enough—most guests expect to receive a paper invitation and RSVP card, and they don't consider your wedding link to be their go-to for information. This chapter tells you *exactly* what information needs to be included in the packet. Mailing out this information will save you so many individual emails and calls with questions from guests that it is literally *priceless!*

Save-the-Dates

Have you already picked out an adorable save-the-date magnet that you're dying to send your guests? Go for it. They're cute and will likely spend the next six months on your guests' refrigerators as a reminder to them. Since you're DIYing, you probably have a fun theme in mind. Kick it off by sending a date announcement that sets the tone for your wedding. Make sure you're comfortable with the guest list before you start mailing anything out, because once a guest has been included on the save-the-date list, they're yours through the RSVP.

All a save-the-date needs to say is when and where you're getting married. You might note there is a "travel information packet" to follow, so they can keep an eye out. But all you're doing with the first mailing is notifying everybody that you actually do have a date now, and you want them to be ready to buy plane tickets! The more notice you give guests for a destination wedding, the more likely they are to attend. Remember, people need to take time off from work and make childcare arrangements, not just shop for a fun dress to wear to your wedding. For a destination wedding, save-the-dates may be sent as early as two years ahead of the actual wedding date, although eighteen months is more realistic. If you're planning on a short timeline, save-the-dates buy you another couple of weeks to get all the information together that you must include in the travel information packet.

Making a Travel Information Packet that Actually Helps Your Guests

While save-the-dates are cute, travel information packets are far more important and should contain every bit of information your invitees need in order to make a decision about whether they can actually attend your wedding.

Actually Getting Your Guests There

You can recommend a travel agent if you have somebody that you've used forever and really like and trust, but you absolutely, positively should not enter into any group travel contracts for your wedding guests. Your guests are all adults. They have their preferred airlines. You'll recommend accommodations, but they *don't have to do anything* they don't want to do. They're going to stay where they want to stay.

Don't try to negotiate group airline travel for your guests unless you're a masochist. DIYing your wedding doesn't have to mean you provide services for your guests that no other bride and groom feel compelled to do. It simply means you're coordinating the planning of your own wedding. None of the airlines will do easy discounts for your guests anymore. American Airlines was the last one to give out group codes that allowed guests to save money flying to your destination from anywhere during a pre-established two-week window around your wedding. When they merged with

US Airways, the wedding group discount codes were one of those great things that got destroyed in the merger.

Almost all airlines require you to commit to a specific number of seats, and everybody has to fly the same itinerary. This means your guests won't have any flexibility to turn your destination wedding into their own vacation. Unless you have somebody who has a hookup, stay out of the travel-booking business for your guests. You have enough on your plate already without having to deal with that nightmare. It's a far better idea to simply tell your guests how to get where they're going and then sit back and let them make their own decisions.

Be sure to include every step of the travel needed to get to your destination. For example, when guests are traveling to Puerto Rico for weddings on Vieques or Culebra Island, everyone needs to fly into San Juan International Airport. But from San Juan, there are several options to get the guests from there to the smaller islands.

In travel info packets for my clients, I always tell guests there are three different ways to get from the big island to the little islands, and they each take three different amounts of time and cost three different amounts of money. And then we provide the different puddle-jumper airline options as well as the ferry option, explaining how to get to each and the nuances involved with each of the choices. For example, you can't bring a rental car on the ferry, and you need to arrive at the ferry terminal at least an hour ahead of the boat you're planning to catch in order to be assured you'll get a ticket. And always buy a roundtrip ferry ticket so you won't have to rush and worry when you're headed back home.

If you're getting married someplace that requires a multi-step travel process, you have to explain it clearly and *make it seem easy,* or some of your guests will be turned off or frightened away. And you do want your guests to accept your invitation, right? So you have to make everything as crystal clear as possible for them.

If your destination can be reached by car or plane from the main airport, provide all of that detailed information—including the driving directions—for your guests in the initial packet. For some guests, knowing they can rent a car with some other friends attending, and share the expense to get from point B (the major airport) to point C (where you're getting married), may be the difference between whether or not they accept your invitation. Kicking in $100 towards the car rental versus buying a $250 plane ticket is a huge difference to some guests, especially if they're traveling with a family. While you're doing them a lovely favor by including children (if you did), they're honoring you tremendously by spending whatever it costs to haul a family of five to your remote destination wedding. The very least you can do is provide all the travel alternatives you can come up with in your own research. And once you've been there on your scouting trip, you'll have additional insight to contribute—for example, don't take the ferry if you have a tendency to get seasick, because it's a rough ride, or be aware that little airlines have planes that only seat seven people, or you need a four-wheel-drive vehicle because of the snow that time of year at the destination.

Some destinations require multiple flights. There are few places down-island in the Caribbean that can be reached directly from any city in the United States. Be clear about where to go for what. They may have to fly into San Juan and take another plane to St. Thomas to catch the ferry to St. John, if they couldn't get something straight into St. Thomas (most can't). Explain these details, provide contact information for the most reliable airlines, and provide every little detail about taking the ferry to your destination. Without this information provided to them, some guests will simply do one online search and decide it's too difficult. You need to make it seem easy.

Accommodation Recommendations

Where you tell your guests to stay depends entirely on the wedding venue you have selected at your destination. If you're at a large hotel with a room block to fill, you might want to tell all your guests to stay there. If you don't satisfy the minimum for the room block, most hotels will make you pay the difference. Consider that carefully before you make a commitment that your friends will have to keep for you. Some of your guests may go off the reservation and search for private rentals on VRBO.com or HomeAway.com—but your first obligation is to fill up your venue.

Big hotels will give you a process to share with your guests for how to book rooms in your block—sometimes even providing a private website portal just for them. That doesn't mean you can sit back and ignore the progress of the reservations, especially if you have a certain number of rooms blocked and have to release the extras by a certain date.

If you're using a boutique hotel or guesthouse with a limited number of rooms that you still have to completely fill, you might assign those rooms to your immediate family and wedding party and suggest alternative accommodations nearby (which of course you scoped out when you visited) for everybody else. Ask the hotel to give you a room chart with what rooms are where and how much each costs, and then use common sense to assign the rooms. This is when you might discuss in advance with some single friends whether they want to share or have their own room.

Provide the property with a list of names of the people who will be staying with you so that they are prepared when your guests call to make their reservations. If you are assigning *all* of the rooms at the specific wedding venue, don't even list that property on the accommodations list in the general travel info packet. Instead, include a separate slip of paper in the travel info packet with their name on it that says something like "a room has been reserved for you at the hotel where the wedding is being held, so that you may stay with the wedding party. Please contact so-and-so to make your reservation by the following date." Be sure to let them know if there is a particular discount code to refer to when making their reservations.

With that said, don't trust everybody to make reservations in a timely manner. You'll have to stay on top of that process after the formal invitations have gone out, checking in with the hotel to see how many rooms have actually been booked. More than one couple has had to eat the cost of empty rooms they weren't anticipating when their invitees didn't follow instructions. This happened to clients of mine when the Mother of the Groom decided to rent a private villa and bring all her family along to villas nearby after the bride had asked the hotel to block rooms for them. Several guests who were going to villas cancelled reservations at the hotel where the wedding was being held. The bride and groom ended up paying for three empty rooms at the venue. Make sure the people assigned to rooms at your venue understand you're counting on them to actually stay there.

For the rest of your guests, provide a variety of different price-points for accommodations options. Some people want a posh hotel and require Wi-Fi and room service to survive. Other guests would prefer to rent a private house or condo for their stay. Some just want to stay someplace that has kitchen facilities or a fridge in the room so they don't have to eat every meal out for the entire trip. The cost of the room per night makes a huge difference for many guests as to whether they just spend the weekend or get to enjoy a full week away.

Provide Internet links to the accommodations you're recommending, as well as telephone numbers and detailed descriptions of the places if you have that information. Don't make anything up or sugarcoat anything, or you could end up with unhappy campers after they arrive to find out there's no TV or air-conditioning someplace you called "adorable" or "quaint." Seasoned budget travelers know what they're looking for and will check TripAdvisor.com to make sure they find it.

Transportation at the Destination

Some destinations don't have public transportation available. Some hotels don't offer any shuttles. Until just recently, the island where I'm based didn't have a real taxi service, just "publico" vans that were very unreliable after about nine o'clock in the evening. In some destinations, all of your guests will need to get rental cars. In other places, they'll be picked up at the airport by shuttle and returned the same way, and they only need a taxi or rental car if they plan to go exploring on their own time off the property.

If everybody needs to get a rental car, look into getting a discounted rate for your group if everybody rents from the same rental car company. If no discount is available, give your guests all of the options and let them figure out whether they want to rent an SUV or convertible for their vacation. It's their money to spend—you just need to point them in the right direction. But tell them *on no uncertain terms* that everybody has to have a rental car to get around at the destination or you'll find yourself in a real pickle when it's time to get your guests somewhere off-site for a wedding activity. I've seen grooms miss an entire pig roast party while they ferried guests to the beach one load at a time from all over our island. Do not let your guests turn you into their chauffeur.

They're adults. Give them the information and if, God forbid, they ignore you and don't arrange a way to get around, simply provide the best taxi info you can and let it go. You will not work so hard to DIY every aspect of your wedding, only to spend the entire weekend catering to those who could not follow simple instructions.

Tentative Itinerary of Events

Remember, the game plan is to send out the travel info packets as fast as you can gather the correct information for their trips. That doesn't mean you have to be committed to every aspect of your wedding events when you send them. In fact, you might still be making major decisions. And some of them are based on your budget and won't get locked in until you have a real head count of those who accepted the invitation.

It's okay not to know everything when you send this initial information to your guests, as long as you're telling them when they need to arrive and how long they need to stay. It's fine, for example, to write "Thursday Night: Welcome Party—Location and Time TBA." More importantly, if you intend to have events the day after your wedding but just haven't locked in the what and where, be sure to indicate that on your tentative itinerary so your guests know not to book flights out the first thing the next morning. Most of them won't want to miss anything after travelling so far to celebrate with you. But you can't wait until a month before your wedding to announce new activity plans before and after the wedding that likely conflict with the travel arrangements of a bunch of guests. People will feel bitter about missing things because you weren't courteous enough to give them a heads-up before they booked their plane tickets that can't be changed without spending a lot more money.

When Should You Send Out the Travel Information?

If your destination wedding is less than a year away, get those travel info packets in the mail immediately. The more lead time people have to research the trip before needing to respond to your RSVP, the more guests who will accept your invitation.

In a perfect world, if you're mailing your invitations to your destination wedding within a year of the wedding, you should send out save-the-dates as soon as you have your wedding venue under contract. Following the save-the-dates, the travel info packets should arrive two to three weeks later, and then put the actual invitations in the mail to your guests a few weeks after that.

Why Not Just Use a Wedding Website for Everything?

Not all of your guests will bother to click on the link to your wedding website when they get the email about your wedding. Unless the email specifically alerts them that they won't be receiving any snail mail about the wedding (and they actually read *that part* of the message), a bunch of your invitees won't bother to look at a wedding website.

Relying solely on Internet communication for your wedding information is a dangerous prospect that usually ends up costing you a lot of time and frustration down the road. I do think making your own web page is a great idea, and I recommend you put everything in your travel info packet on that page, but you cannot count on a wedding website to do all your communication for you. The result will be countless phone calls and emails for information you've already provided by people who didn't click on every link of the page, if they bothered to go there at all. Trust me, this is one time that it's well worth the effort to put something in a real mailbox.

You do not have to hand-address save-the-dates or travel information packets—it's perfectly acceptable to print out attractive mailing labels and save yourselves a bunch of time. Just make sure you get all the salutations right when you set up the spreadsheet of guests from the very beginning. That guest list you've created will become an incredibly helpful tool as you make your way down the path of wedding planning.

Destination Wedding Invitations

You can mail your destination wedding invitations as far out as *one year before* your wedding. A lot of my clients have gotten a kick out of putting them in the mail on the actual date of the one-year-out mark and waiting to see who notices that little detail.

Traditional wedding invitations are optional these days—meaning you don't have to use just plain ivory or white paper stock (you have a rainbow of options), and nobody even bothers with engraving anymore. Your wedding invitation may reflect the theme of the wedding or your individual personalities, if you so desire. However, the information you collect on the RSVP card is very, very important for your sanity.

Destination Wedding RSVP Additions

You will choose whatever standard wedding phraseology you prefer, such as "accepts with pleasure" or "declines with regret," but you also need to add a few extra lines for a destination wedding.

Ask the guests "Where are you staying?" and "When are you arriving?" to save yourself a whole lot of time when you're creating your welcome bag delivery list closer to your wedding date. If you know your menu options for the reception dinner and need to collect those orders in advance, go ahead and add that to the RSVP as well. You don't even have to be specific—in fact, traditionally you're not supposed to be—just ask them if they want beef, fish, or vegetarian, or whatever you're planning to offer for dinner. It doesn't matter if you haven't chosen the final menu yet, but you'll have to stay within the protein parameters you've offered to your guests.

Addressing Your Wedding Invitations

Traditionally, wedding invitations should be hand-addressed, and I believe this is an important custom. For hard-core destination DIYers who want to do all the cutting, gluing, stamping, and bow-tying with their own hands, this should be a fun project. The bride and groom should ask their moms to help, or you can invite your besties who have the nicest handwriting and set up an assembly line. Stuffing those suckers takes time too! If you must have calligraphy, either buy yourself a fancy pen and practice to ensure you'll be happy with the results, or contact a calligrapher at the same time you order your invitations to get on their schedule. With that said, you wanted to do it yourself, right? Beautifully addressing your own wedding invitations is well worth the effort and saves a lot of money.

If you're super artsy and have DIY'd the actual invitations, you can begin addressing them as soon as you complete some of them, starting with the people you know you will definitely be inviting. Ideally, you had your guest list nailed down before you started creating your invitations, but if you're hand-making every aspect of them, you have a little more flexibility.

Be sure to take an invitation to the post office ahead of time (whether you made them or ordered them) and check to make sure the dimensions and weight of the envelope and its contents fall within the specifications of a regular first-class postage stamp. Many wedding invitations require additional postage if they're more creative or include heavier inserts. Ask your post office if they have "wedding stamps." The US Postal Service does several runs of wedding-themed stamps every year, from linked rings to pretty bouquets. It's a fun addition to an already beautiful invitation, and it doesn't cost you a penny extra to choose a cute stamp for both your invitations and your RSVP envelopes.

A Word on Doing Online Invitations

Although the times are changing and many of us receive social invitations to events via Evite or Facebook, that's not the best way to handle your wedding invitations. Consider why you're even thinking about keeping it online before you make a decision. Are you doing it because you're lazy? Probably not, or you wouldn't be DIYing in the first place. But if your reason is that you think that it will make your life *easier*, guess again.

As I just explained to you, a lot of people don't even look at wedding websites they receive in their email. Why? Because they assume the information will also be coming via snail mail and they don't find you nearly as fascinating as you find yourselves. I'm not kidding. Many wedding websites are completely nauseating, with endless pictures of the couple and the story of their lives. That's fine if you want to include all of that information on a website that may or may not be totally secure, but if you load it up like that, a lot of guests will click and look for twenty seconds before they say "whatever" and move on to the next project in their pile. Again, it's not that they don't love you or care about your wedding, but they just expect that you will do the "normal" thing and send them an actual invitation, along with any other pertinent information they need to have.

When you create your wedding web page, be sure to password protect it—and not with your names or the name of your destination. Identity theft from websites is simply too easy for the bad guys. Especially if you've included everything from the story of when you first met to pictures of all the places you've celebrated your birthdays together. If you've been very detailed, a good identity thief can get your address, birth dates, mothers' maiden names, and the list of your wedding party all in one place. Not only can somebody practically get a loan in your name with that information, but you're compromising the security of everybody identified on that page as a guest, family member, or wedding party by basically announcing to the world when you're all going to be out of town. Bad idea.

Please don't misunderstand my guidance here—I think having all your important wedding details and travel information posted someplace your guests can quickly access it online is a really great idea. I just want you to be very careful how you post, what you post, and who can see it.

Collecting the RSVPs

Wouldn't it be nice if everybody could do the courteous thing and actually take the little card you've provided, put it into the pre-addressed, pre-stamped envelope you sent along with the invitation, and drop it in the mail? Sadly, they won't. All brides and grooms have a handful of MIAs a week after the RSVP deadline. How aggressive you have to be in following up with these people has a lot to do with how much time is left before your wedding. As a general rule, you have every right to begin stalking them within a couple of weeks.

A polite email making sure they received the invitation is the first step, and definitely implies you didn't receive an RSVP. If you don't hear back, the next move is a phone call—not a text—where your real voice talks to their real voice and asks if they are planning to attend your wedding. If the offenders are relatives of one of you, that's the lucky person who gets to make the phone call. If it's someone invited by either set of your parents, you can totally dump that task on them and make them get the response.

Because destination wedding invites go out so much earlier than invitations for a wedding at home, you have a little more wiggle room in your follow-up time. But not much. Allowing your guests to drag their feet on responding to your invitation will put your schedule for other things behind, because you won't know how many people you're going to be paying for at the actual wedding. No matter how uncomfortable it feels to push to get an answer, try to remember that you are not the one who is being rude—they are. All they had to do was mail back the RSVP.

Reality Check: If they can't say they're coming when you personally contact them to ask, they're not coming. Seriously. They just don't know how to tell you that. So your job at this point is to tell them you have a deadline for your headcount and need an answer, and you're very sorry if that means they won't be able to join you. For somebody who is being lazy, it will kick them in the butt to buy a plane ticket and commit. You're letting the ones who didn't have the guts to tell you they weren't coming off the hook when you essentially un-invite them because they never accepted the invitation.

No matter what anybody tries to tell you to the contrary, you should mail your destination wedding invitations as soon as possible after the one-year-out mark. The more lead time you give your guests, the higher the likelihood they'll be able to attend. It also shows you're being thoughtful and courteous about your guests' schedules and their need to plan and budget ahead.

CHAPTER 8

∽◯◯∼

FINDING VENDORS AND DEALING WITH VENDORS AT YOUR DESTINATION

*Y*ou've chosen a wedding destination someplace fabulous and you've found just the right venue for your big day. You've got the invitation process rolling with save-the-dates and travel information and, hopefully, you've got a real wedding invitation in the printing works. Now it's time to actually put your wedding together.

If you've purchased a wedding package at a hotel or resort, they are probably taking care of a lot of your arrangements—but not all. You must get an explicit list from them of what they will, and what they won't, do for you. Most hotels will provide a list of recommended vendors (and required vendors—some hotels will only work with specific businesses they've approved). Just because a vendor is recommended doesn't mean they're the best person for the job—you have to do your own research on each and every one you consider hiring. Reach out to former clients if you're able to identify them. A vendor with a listing on WeddingWire.com or another reputable site is probably a safe bet if they've got *real* reviews posted. You can tell the difference after you've read through a few—real reviews include significantly more personal detail than those posted by imaginary clients. Look for *real* pictures and *real* video so you can scope out their services in action. A music vendor, for example, should have some YouTube videos posted that you can watch, and a pastry chef should have a website or extensive social media pages showcasing his or her work. There are always some exceptions to the rule—but for the most part, *experienced* destination wedding vendors realize they have to provide something for potential clients to look at, so finding them isn't that difficult. It's getting them to call you or respond to your email that can be tricky.

Cultural Differences between Stateside and Other Wedding Vendors

If you are DIYing your wedding someplace in the continental United States, you should absolutely, positively expect a regular (or better) level of responsiveness from any potential vendor you contact. They should respond to you within forty-eight hours, unless you've sent your email to them on a Friday afternoon. Remember, good wedding vendors are absolutely slammed from Friday through Sunday because they have clients they are servicing, and the best vendors will not take their focus off a current client to respond to an inquiry from a bride or groom who might *potentially* hire them. When they get their head above water, you will hear back, probably with an apology for the delay in responding to your initial inquiry.

Unfortunately, what's considered a "timely" response to a vendor inquiry in the continental United States is not the standard the minute you go outside it—even if you're going to Hawaii, Puerto Rico, or the US Virgin Islands. "Island time" is not merely an expression—it is a way of life. Many of the wedding vendors you're contacting in the Caribbean or in Latin America are not full-time wedding vendors. They do what they do—food, music, hair, cakes, etc.—all the time and wedding clients just happen to be one small piece of their bread and butter.

There's a completely different mentality down here in the Caribbean, where my husband likes to joke that in Puerto Rico, "mañana does not mean tomorrow, it just means not today!" He's totally right. When we've pressured different vendors for an exact time for a response to a question or problem, we've even heard the following: "Mañana . . . or mañana mañana." What the hell does that mean? I've learned it means tomorrow or the next day or whenever they get around to it.

Lots of DIY brides contact me when they've already started planning their destination weddings because, after countless hours of research and preparation, *nobody* on their must-have vendor list of the people who are supposedly "the best" is actually calling them back. And they don't understand why that is. If somebody is the best wedding vendor of something at a particular location, wouldn't they know how to check their voicemail? To somebody from the States, especially a bride from a major city with a fast-paced job, the responsiveness, or lack thereof, is more than disconcerting—it freaks them out completely. It can take a completely determined-to-DIY bride to the emotional edge and drive her to call a wedding planner. That doesn't necessarily mean they end up hiring me every time. But all of those kinds of panicked and confused calls are part of what inspired me to write this book. If you're going to DIY your wedding someplace where people don't habitually wear watches, you need to be prepared for a bit of culture shock.

Here's the really important thing to understand—you cannot get rude about the response time when you are trying to find destination wedding vendors. The vast majority of these people do not care whether or not they get your business. I know it's completely counterintuitive to think that a vendor of any kind, anywhere, wouldn't care if you hire them or not, but that's the reality, especially in Latin America and the tropics. The native local vendors have been functioning quite well for their entire lives without asking brides and grooms how high they are expected to jump—that's not their way of doing business. If you push too hard, they will simply choose not to work with you. As a wedding planner, this is absolutely infuriating to me because I have to be the bridge between the frustrated client and the island vendor. Let me give you an example of how one of my brides disregarded my advice on this.

Burning Bridges

When I started my business on Vieques in 2007, there were only about five legitimate car rental companies (none of them a national brand) and then there were also a handful of off-the-record car rental operators you could turn to when you needed a car. These tended to be the less expensive ones, since they're operating off-the-books and without all the proper paperwork. When my husband and I first bought our Vieques house, we found out that a small legit company run by a neighbor was really reasonably priced. When I started planning weddings on Vieques Island professionally in 2007, his car rental was at the top of my recommendations list.

The only problem was that he didn't book rentals a year in advance—to this day we question exactly how his rental system works, but it does—and so when couples called him to book a car, it was not uncommon to be told to call back in a few months. This doesn't sit well with anxious brides, so I quickly moved him to the bottom of the recommendations list (but didn't delete him) and made it clear to my brides that they would probably never get a return call from him—if he doesn't answer, just try him again a few hours later—and the fact that he didn't require a deposit shouldn't freak them out as long as he gave them a confirmation when they did book the reservation.

Unfortunately, one of my all-time favorite clients didn't listen to my instructions when it came to booking cars from this guy. In her head, she wanted to reserve *all* of his cars for her guests; therefore, he should have responded to the messages she left him regarding car rental reservations for her wedding more than a year in the future. When she dogged him for a week and emailed me to complain about it, I reiterated my instructions. I told her to wait six months to follow up with him and if she couldn't do that, go ahead and make reservations someplace else, as long as she wouldn't lose money on a deposit if she cancelled six months later in favor of using my neighbor's company. I was really, really explicit, and I didn't give it another thought.

The bride emailed me a week or so later telling me that her mother had taken over the car rental responsibilities and she couldn't get a call back from this particular car rental either. I groaned aloud at my desk, just imagining the look on my neighbor's face when he got bombed with a whole new round of calls from the same wedding group wanting to book his cars. It also sounded as though the Mother of the Bride might have been getting progressively nastier in her messages as she got more frustrated. I replied to the bride and her mom, who was cc'd on the email, and told them again to *back off* for six months and try then if they really wanted to rent his cars. But it was too late.

A few days later, I ran into my neighbor on our street and mentioned, in an apologetic tone, that one of my brides had confessed to harassing him a little bit, and that I was sorry and had told her to call him closer to her wedding date. He was polite, but he was direct.

"Sandy, I don't mind renting cars to people who are here for weddings, but I don't really care if they're here for weddings or just on vacation. I don't think I want to work with your brides anymore. It's not personal and I'll still rent cars to you and Bill, but please don't ask those crazy girls to call me anymore."

One overly enthusiastic bride and I had lost a vendor—one whom I actually had a personal, neighborly friendship with. I was horrified and pissed. I sent the bride and her mother an email (after sleeping on the first draft I'd written, which is always a good idea when you're really angry at someone) the next morning telling them they were no longer able to even consider renting from this company and should go ahead and choose another car rental. And then I had to email all of my clients who already had the information about the car rental and tell them that although they could certainly continue to give the information to their guests in their travel info packets for planning purposes, guests *should not* reference their wedding or Weddings in Vieques when making a reservation. I was specific. I told them why. While I didn't name and shame the bride who had broken the guidelines for dealing with our local vendors, I made it clear that the actions of one bride could, in fact, have a really serious impact on every other wedding taking place on the island.

This particular vendor experience was the impetus for beginning a client guide we send to all of our brides and grooms. It's informational, but it also has quite a lot of "thou shalt nots" in it that make some of my couples think I'm a little crazy. But it's not just the "native" local vendors who get irritated with demanding brides—it's almost everybody. So now, eight years later, that client guide is more than forty pages long, and each and every item in it is a direct result of something our clients repeatedly did and had to be educated about so it wouldn't keep happening. I had to address it thoroughly so that I wouldn't keep losing vendors. The following is an excerpt from my actual client guide:

Dealing with Local Vendors and Local Business Culture

Reality Check: *None of the vendors on Vieques do weddings here because we're desperate for your money.* We could all be making more money doing the exact same thing back wherever we came from. Our choice to live and work in Vieques is a quality of life decision. And nobody here has any desire to work with difficult or nasty clients.

It's a good idea to be nice and friendly to everybody we work with down here during the course of planning your wedding. "Bridezillas" don't go over well on Vieques. It's a small island. If you behave badly during your planning process, everybody will dread your arrival when your wedding week finally comes. I'm not saying this to threaten you, but rather to give you an idea of the culture of the island.

In Vieques, "mañana" doesn't mean tomorrow, it just means "not today." A vendor who says he'll get back to us "mañana" means he'll be in touch when he can answer our questions or has a proposal for us. And he will. If he needs a little prodding, that's my job. If you ask me to prod him and I say I already have, I need you to back off and chill out a bit while we wait for him to get back to me. If you call him, or have the groom call him, or have your mom call him and bug him after I've already done it, it will not go over well. I've had a few clients who have bugged vendors until they refused to have anything to do with the couple's wedding at all. That upsets the bride, it upsets the groom because the bride is upset, and it upsets me because you've just made it harder for me to get what I need from this vendor for future brides. Don't spoil it for everyone! There are a limited number of people who do the things you need for your wedding. Believe me—if we're running out of time I'll go sit on the guy til we get what we need. But until then, leave the worrying to me and relax.

Because you don't actually have a wedding planner or advocate at your destination to help you with this process, DIYers need to start their planning very early in order to avoid panicking about the delayed responses, or your entire planning experience will be a nightmare and put a damper on the overall wedding. And you won't get the vendors you really want if you harass the crap out of them before they've even gotten a deposit from you.

Figuring Out What Vendors You Need

As I said earlier in this chapter, if you're getting married at a larger hotel or resort, they'll likely give you a list of recommended vendors. DIY brides and grooms who have rented private villas or small boutique hotels or guest houses have to find it all themselves. Finding the destination's local publication online and seeing advertisements for some vendors who say they do weddings is a good start, but you have to research them all as carefully as you would a dog sitter caring for your much-loved pet. Anyone in the world can create a website, buy advertising space in a local publication, or list themselves on a wedding vendor website. It's peeling back the layers of the onion to find out if they're legit, reliable, and good that takes a lot more time, but it's mission critical and worth the effort.

Almost every DIY wedding couple must track down the vast majority of the following vendors: minister, caterer, service staff (if not provided by the caterer), musicians, pastry chef, flower supplier (or actual florist if you're not wanting to DIY your bouquets and other flowers), rental equipment, linens, lighting, transportation, hairdresser, makeup artist, and many more. Depending on your particular needs, you might also have to find *safe* babysitters, people to help with setup and cleanup, information about the permit processes for holding events in specific locations at your destination, and many more things that you don't even realize you'll need until you're three-quarters into the planning process.

Checking Vendor References

Start with all the online information that you've dug up about your destination. Cross-reference the names of the vendors on reputable wedding websites and determine whom you're most impressed with at the outset. If they don't have enough information online for you to feel secure about their professional history, try to reach out to previous clients on your own *before* you actually contact the vendor. You should also ask them for references, but you have no way of knowing if you're talking to a real former bride of theirs or if you're talking to a cousin who has been prepped to take your call and swear that hairdresser or pastry chef walks on water.

If you're contacting references provided by the vendors, please try to talk to the former clients on the telephone directly. Ask them to send you some of their wedding pictures to check out if you get a good feeling about the call. Normal brides and grooms can shoot off an email to you immediately with a few of their faves. It's not a bad idea to insert a bit of urgency into your request so that you can see how long it takes them to respond. If you initially emailed them and set up a call and they were really fast to reply with all of that, but then they take forever to send you pictures, and the pictures make you wonder if it was really their wedding, trust your gut instinct and find somebody else. That's a sign they've called their cousin to find out what to send you to continue the ruse that they were actual clients.

Working with Less Experienced Vendors

Sometimes you will encounter a new vendor who doesn't have a whole lot of former clients or loads of pictures to show you, simply because they're new to the business. Or all they can send you are pictures of weddings they've planned elsewhere, because they're new at your destination. It's much better to use a longer-established vendor than a newbie, but sometimes the new guy is your only option. You shouldn't automatically eliminate new vendors, but you should dig a little deeper and expect those vendors to be willing to answer more questions and supply more information than you would somebody who has an obvious five or more years of experience at the destination.

New vendors are often less expensive, because they're trying to get their first clients so they can establish themselves and have good legitimate testimonials to post. Sure, you're taking a bit of a chance, but DIYing a destination is taking a really big chance on your really big day, so in the grand scope of things, this isn't a deal breaker.

Be more thorough in reviewing contracts and service agreements, and don't hesitate to ask for changes (they may still be figuring out the contract process on their end or used to dealing with wedding planners who provide the paperwork). Delay your initial deposits and final payments as far out as you can on the contract, although you want to be sure to make the payments on time. Try to pay by credit card if possible because it gives you more protection (unfortunately, most newer vendors often don't take credit cards). Get confirmation in writing of all payments and communicate more frequently with a newish vendor than you would with someone who has been the top wedding cake baker in your destination for the past ten years.

As a hard rule, I *never ever* use a vendor who hasn't been physically at that destination for at least a year unless there truly is no other option. Even with established vendors (not counting actual villas or venues), don't start paying deposits until the one-year-out mark. You can be working on your catering menu and get a bid and start the contract process rolling, but turnover in the islands and many other tourist destinations is uniquely fast. Unfortunately, I have seen more advertised wedding vendors appear and then disappear in fewer than six months than you can even imagine. Do your research, and you can avoid having this happen as much as possible.

Meeting with Your Vendors in Person

DIYers who can afford to visit their destination after they've selected their wedding venue have the very best odds of getting good, legitimate vendors signed on to execute their destination wedding.

There are, though, a few things to keep in mind before you book your travel plans. No, it's *not* the same as back in the continental United States, in that you probably can't do a free tasting of your wedding food, if they offer tastings at all. It's also really unlikely that you can do a traditional cake tasting like back up north, because most of the pastry chefs work from their homes and don't keep a full stash of all their flavors ready for you to sample and gush over. While you'd think it might be worth the effort for them to get your business, it's really not. Most destination clients do not go to their destinations to select the littlest details in person, and so vendors aren't prepared. Many caterers don't have actual restaurants and would have to custom-order the ingredients for your wish list just for the tasting.

But that doesn't mean you shouldn't try to meet with your vendors if you can. A couple using a professional planner can trust their planner's recommendations without worrying too much—a wedding planner wouldn't be in business for long if he or she recommended lousy vendors—but a DIY wedding couple who can meet face-to-face with vendors ahead of time will worry a lot less if they get a good vibe and a sense of professionalism from somebody they meet with in person. You know how they say that you can't judge a hairdresser by his/her own haircut because he/she didn't cut it? That's not true of wedding vendors. If you're interviewing a stylist who will be spending the day with your bridal party in close quarters, and she shows up to meet with you initially in ratty clothing, hair a mess, and doesn't bring the pictures she promised, run like hell. Not only is she demonstrating a total lack of professionalism, which will do nothing to assuage your fears about whether she's the one you want doing your hair on your wedding day, but she'll also probably show up in the background of your dressing photos (looking just as bad) as she finishes your hair and makeup.

Years ago, my beauty team's head stylist came to me and asked if her team could wear Weddings in Vieques uniforms when they did hair and makeup. I was surprised they'd want to, but I was flattered and said yes. Yaya had always dressed professionally and so had everybody working for her, and while I was happy to slap my logo all over them, it wasn't necessary. She explained her reasoning and I groaned because it made perfect sense. She had a very talented new girl who could do fabulous wedding hair, but she had a *lot* of very visible tattoos and her clothing choices were, at best, questionable. Yaya figured that if she could cover up (for the most part) anything that might turn off a more conservative client, the girl would be stellar at her job. And she was right. With her whole team in our uniform shirts, you barely noticed all the ink on that particular member of her group. When I ran into the young lady on a Friday night dressed in her own choice of clothing, I didn't even recognize her. Good call, Yaya!

My point is that when you meet with vendors, their appearance should mean something to you. A chef in a filthy outfit isn't acceptable, unless he's meeting with you briefly right after a meal service to accommodate your schedule, and clearly wouldn't have had time to change and clean up his act. When you meet at a reasonable, non-rushed time, caterers should appear to be organized, clean, and professional. If they meet with you dressed in a way that makes you think "ick," imagine what your guests will think when they see him cooking their dinner.

Making Sure Your Vendors Are Legal

You might not think it matters if your wedding vendors are completely "legal" at your destination . . . but do your research. You especially can't mess around with the bigger items like the rental equipment company and the caterers. You should ask these vendors if they have insurance and if they have legal permits to do business at the destination. If you get the slightest hinky feeling, you should ask for proof. If they're legit and they want your business, they'll send you something to demonstrate they are registered, have their health certificates, and that everything else is in order. If they don't send it to you (especially after you've sent them a polite reminder requesting it again), odds are they don't have it, and you have to decide whether you feel comfortable turning over your hard-earned dollars to this person in the form of a deposit when you have no legal recourse if something goes wrong.

Too many caterers do not have liquor licenses for the booze at your wedding. Many won't bother to get the proper beach permits or other necessary paperwork to execute your event in the location you've chosen, and some of them won't even bother to mention that it was necessary. It's an ugly scene when the police show up and tell you that you must shut down an event because you didn't have the proper paperwork that you didn't even know about.

Find out What Permits Are Required for Your Events

What follows is a true story about securing permits that will make every DIY bride and groom cringe. I was contacted by a sweet couple who wanted to hire me to plan their destination wedding a year later. But I was right in the middle of filming my TLC show "Wedding Island" and executing two weddings a week, so I didn't have much time to chat. I did a brief consultation and even came up with a super-cool idea of having their wedding at a very special shallow beach on paddleboards because they'd joked that was their ideal way to get married. I was totally on board with it (pun intended) and assured them I knew it could be done and exactly how. There were only a few beaches that would work, but it could really be done.

They were enthusiastic and wanted to do another consultation to hire me and go to contract, and I wanted them to hire me. But we were filming two weddings a week, I was only sleeping four or five nights a week, and I wasn't allowed to do any non-show client work while they were filming, which was approximately eighteen hours a day. I had scheduled all of my new potential clients for follow-up consultations a few weeks later if they weren't absolutely ready to sign a contract or getting married the next month. Most of those couples understood and appreciated my honesty. This couple was seriously miffed. So instead of patiently waiting to talk to me (their wedding date was almost eighteen months in the future), they found another wedding planner and hired her instead. And when I followed up after filming to schedule a call, they sent me a nasty-gram and told me they'd hired somebody cheaper while I was too busy for them.

I'd completely forgotten about the paddleboard couple until more than a year later, when they actually got married on Vieques with a less-than-professional wedding planning team. Apparently my "competition" sucked. The planners didn't get the right permits for the right beach with calm shallow water, so they told the couple they'd have to have the ceremony on Sun Bay. The water is a lot deeper there and there can be some real waves, but I believe the switch was made at the last minute and the couple didn't have much opportunity to check out what they had agreed to.

While my plan of using the shallow-watered Media Luna beach would have been perfect, Sun Bay was not conducive to letting the photographers roam around in water up to their thighs to take pictures of the ceremony from all directions. They could only shoot from the beach side. But that wasn't the worst part. Even though *everybody* knows you have to get permits for commercial activities on Sun Bay, the planners hadn't gotten them. Also, that beach is governed by the Puerto Rico Department of Natural Resources, and they don't permit any flotation devices to be used at commercial events (the logic behind it is completely flawed, but it is a law and one of the few they actually enforce). Paddleboards are definitely considered flotation devices.

Essentially, this couple was having an illegal, unpermitted wedding ceremony and breaking other laws in the process. They probably had no idea, but their wedding planners should have. If you're DIYing your wedding, you have to research the permit requirements, rules, restrictions, and actual laws that apply to the particular venue at your destination. You can't just decide to get married at a lighthouse, or what appears to be an old abandoned church, without contacting the local municipality to find out what has to be done to have permission to use that location. But I digress . . .

As the story was told to me by another vendor who was there, the minister, who happens to be a professional paddleboarder (if there's such a thing), had trouble keeping his footing as they started the ceremony. It was windy and the water was far too whipped up for something as technical as performing a ceremony in five feet of water while standing on a fat surfboard. The couple was having a much tougher time of it. Fortunately, they'd gone the dressed-up bathing suit route and not attempted formal attire on top of water, but it was reportedly painful to watch, according to those who saw the attempt to get the ceremony started. But it didn't matter, because before anything could really get going, they got busted. Not only did the police end the ceremony and basically push them off the beach, but they also reportedly confiscated the paddleboards!

But I didn't tell you that story to mock a wedding catastrophe—I shared it because I want you to understand how destructive the consequences can be to your wedding festivities if you don't make sure that you follow all the rules and regulations wherever you're getting married. This same scenario plays itself out all over, with ceremonies disrupted by officials due to lack of permits or permissions in parks, at monuments, etc. Receptions get shut down by fire marshals for being over capacity. If one of your vendors tells you that you can skip a permit you know you're supposed to get, do not take that advice. Do you really want to risk being the one they make an example out of on your wedding day for a permit that's a couple of hundred dollars?

When you DIY your own wedding, you take on the responsibility of knowing what permits are required for where, and who is going to be responsible for getting them. If your vendor said they'd get them (and especially if they charged you for them), you should ask to see them when you arrive at your destination to make sure they actually exist. It's true you can get away with a lot in the Caribbean—I sincerely doubt most of my "competition" over the years has even had business permits—but if you get caught breaking the rules on your wedding day, it won't matter whose fault it is. Your wedding is still ruined. There are no three-strikes in wedding planning, especially for a DIY bride and groom.

Using a Friend as a Wedding Vendor

Every DIY couple will receive a generous offer of free services as a wedding gift from some friend who has a particular talent or works in the event or catering field. Sometimes it's something easy to accept, but there are some offers that should be declined even if it would save you a lot of money and the effort of finding somebody at your destination.

Hairdressers, makeup artists, and other beauty-type people are a fantastic asset to have as guests at your wedding if they're offering to make you and your wedding party gorgeous on your big day. It saves you *a lot of money* and you can do a practice run (or two) well in advance of your wedding. Accept that offer as fast as you can.

A pastry chef in the family who wants to make your cake or cupcakes is great if you're DIYing at home, but if you're getting married at a destination where the chef doesn't know the oven, and you're not sure which ingredients are available, DIYing a cake can be dicey. We had one client who insisted on having her uncle bake her cupcakes, and he shipped absolutely everything he would need down to the island ahead of his arrival. Now when I say *everything,* I'm not kidding. We do have sugar and flour and other basics available here in Puerto Rico, as I told them. But her uncle liked his particular brands of everything, so he bought it all and put it in the mail. Unfortunately, bags of powdered sugar and flour and God only knows what else exploded en route, and when the mailman delivered them, they were leaking a white powdery substance from every corner. Actually, it was almost comical to imagine how many post offices had been shut down as the package travelled from the West Coast to Puerto Rico (it wasn't that long after the nationwide anthrax scares). And how come the DEA hadn't followed that box right up to our front porch? I assure you the bride and her uncle didn't find the mess as funny as we did. We put the boxes into trash bags to deliver them to their villa when they arrived. Just in case you're curious, the cupcakes turned out fine after he went to our local grocery store to replace a few things. But the frosting slid right off the tops because you can't put that much "butter" in tropical "buttercream" frosting.

Using a Friend as Your Wedding Photographer

Photography is probably the most common, but scariest, wedding gift to accept from a friend who offers to be your official vendor on your wedding day. If it's a good friend whom you want to be part of your wedding party and other festivities, it won't work. They cannot be dancing with you to your favorite song at the same time they are taking pictures of two best friends getting down at a wedding. The result is that you don't get a lot of the important pictures you wanted to document your special day. Trust me, I know. This was my own friend-vendor mistake.

In my case, one of my bridesmaid's husbands was a very talented, wanna-be wedding photographer, and the pictures were their wedding gift to me. I accepted it gleefully because it saved me a ton of money and he was very good. The pictures that he took were absolutely beautiful. But I didn't get all the pictures I wanted. Later on, I learned that I didn't have nearly as many pictures of things as most brides had. When he was dancing with his wife or son (or me), he wasn't taking any pictures of the party going on. And I got married before smart phones, so not as many other folks were taking pictures as you would have nowadays.

If you decide to accept the offer of wedding photography from a friend, you need to sit down and have a very clear conversation about your expectations. You need to let them know at the outset that you greatly appreciate their offer, but if you accept it, you want them to play photographer throughout the entire wedding and reception, not be a regular guest. Make it clear that having them at your wedding is more important than saving the photography money (even if it isn't) and that you'd happily accept the gift of engagement photography instead. If that friend understands what you're saying and suddenly realizes that he or she does actually want to dance and party at your wedding, you're giving them the perfect out and still letting them gift you with photography for another part of your wedding. With that said, if they still want to do your wedding pictures, you've been specific and straightforward about your expectations. And there shouldn't be any misunderstanding or disappointment when you get your pictures back after the wedding.

I do not advise letting a friend who is not actually a wedding photographer take your pictures on your biggest day. It worked out for me (in that the photos were exceptional, if few), but not every kind of photographer knows how to shoot a wedding. They have to get in early to get the detail shots before the guests stick their purses all over your tables. Pictures of the place cards you so lovingly created (and that took hours to glue and label), shots of the favor table, bouquet pictures, and many more little wedding details are not things that somebody who is a career photojournalist or art photographer will necessarily realize that he or she needs to take pictures of, or in what order. If you let somebody make you their wedding experiment, you're really taking a chance. You have to give them a really specific list of shots that you want weeks ahead so you can answer any questions about them. With professional wedding photographers, the only shot list they need is one that consists of things they wouldn't know about, such as pictures of the bride with her sorority sisters, shots of the couple with the kids they grew up with, and his peewee football team buddies. The regular stuff (the detail shots and the formal photos) are things a professional wedding photographer should shoot as a matter of habit. It's one more thing off your to-do list if you don't have to guide your photographer through the how-to-shoot-a-wedding tutorial process.

Think it through carefully before you make a decision, and have that hard conversation with your photographer friend so that you stay friends after the wedding. Some brides would consider it unforgivable if they didn't get every picture they wanted from their wedding day.

DIYing Your Wedding Flowers

YouTube videos make every excited DIY bride *think* she can create her dream bouquet and centerpieces for pennies on the dollar. That's not really true, unless you're planning to practice a lot at home (which requires buying flowers to practice with), and then buying all the supplies you need to make the flowers at your destination. Plus getting it all there. And don't forget the cost of having flowers shipped to your destination—the more remote you are, the pricier it is. If you have girlfriends or a mom who is excited and willing to help make your bouquet, it's easy to get sucked into taking on a really humongous project on your actual wedding weekend.

My first suggestion is that you *hire a professional florist for your destination wedding*. Realize that you don't want to spend the day prior to, and the day of, your wedding dealing with something as time-consuming and important as your bouquets, and spend the

Heather carried a gorgeous combination of blush and ivory roses, ivory mini calla lilies, green Cymbidium orchids (all hand-wired), and hypernicum berries, hand-tied with ivory satin ribbon and featuring a picture of her deceased father as a tribute. She hired my flower shop to make this bouquet. (Photo by Morris Malakoff)

money to hire somebody to do it (if there's actually a florist available at your destination). This is money well spent. To do your own flowers at your destination, you'll need to have *at least* the following items, in addition to the flowers:

- Buckets to hold the flowers in water
- Flower food (can be the difference between life and death, depending on what condition they arrive in—Floralife Quick Dip is amazing, but they're not kidding about the instructions to only submerge the stems for *one second*)
- Air-conditioned place to store them (if you're getting married in the tropics, you'll kill them if you stick them into a fridge after they've been too warm traveling—and who has *that much* spare refrigerator space at their destination wedding venue?)
- Flower scissors (these are not your normal desktop scissors—these will cut through wire ties, sticks, and thick

stems so the bottoms of your bouquets don't appear hacked and shredded)
- Green floral tape
- Rose strippers (for removing the thorns—they make really neat flexible-rubber ones that are easy to use)
- Wire ties (so much easier for quickly tying the stems together than using only floral tape—tape is old-school!)
- Ribbon, lace, floral pins, and anything else you want to wrap around the stems of your bouquets

If you're planning to use orchids or other blooms that require hand-wiring or faux stems, you'll also need to bring water tubes, green sticks, and wire, at least. It's also a really good idea to have a brand-new, unopened tube of floral glue with you, even if you don't think you need it for anything. I've found some very creative ways to save the whole décor using floral glue.

You'll have to figure out who can ship your flowers to your destination wedding location. I have used Potomac Floral Whole-sale, based in Silver Spring, Maryland, as a flower supplier for many years because, although I have some suppliers here in Puerto Rico and using local vendors is cheaper, the quality and reliability of many island suppliers has been inconsistent. I own the flower shop here on the island and I have to make sure that my brides get *exactly* what they want. Close enough isn't good enough. I also like using www.flowerwholesale.com because they have an easy web-site and a full range of floral supplies from wire to ribbon to vases. I can figure out what things cost without waiting for a bid to come back or having to buy anything.

If you find a local supplier that somebody else has recom-mended and you're willing to risk it because you're not that picky about your flowers, check the difference in price and make a decision. If you're spending more and not getting exactly what you want in the name of having "native" flowers in your bouquet, stop right there. Almost all of the world's commercial orchids come from Thailand and most of the roses come from Latin America. Just because you're buying from a local flower supplier doesn't mean you're buying anything grown within a thousand miles of where you're getting married. It's a romantic notion, but it's not reality, and you shouldn't waste one second of your DIY time worrying about a flower's birthplace.

If you're having them shipped in, make sure your flower supplier can actually get those flowers to your destination without killing them. You don't want to be their experiment if they've never shipped to your island before, only to find out the hard way that their shipper only delivers to your destination twice a week. I've lucked out because the general manager at my supplier, Potomac Floral Wholesale, is Puerto Rican—and Andy Pagan has fought with UPS and FedEx (in Spanish) on my behalf at midnight more than once to make sure my flowers got here in time. He actually delivered flowers in person once when he was headed home for a visit.

Trust your supplier's advice regarding the flowers you've chosen for your wedding. Peonies, tulips, ranunculus, poppies, and anemones won't hold up in the Caribbean, for example. Unless you're having your wedding entirely indoors and your flowers will never leave the air-conditioned space, don't even try it. If not for the guidance of my supplier's salesman, Randall Franklin, for many, many years now, I would have had a lot more flower-tastrophies than I've had—and I've had a few. We tried peonies—no bueno. The tulips waited until the bride got to the end of the aisle to actually drop all their petals. Hydrangea, surprisingly, work most of the time if you're keeping them in water in centerpieces. If you use them in your bouquet, they'll make it through the ceremony and pictures but will probably be deader than doornails after that. If you don't plan to repurpose them as décor at your reception, go for it. But order twice as many as you actually need, keep them cold, and spray them constantly with water (add spray bottle to your list of supplies from above). Talk sweetly to them and pray, and maybe two-thirds of them will look good enough to use on your wedding day.

Silk flowers are popular for DIY brides because you can make all of the bouquets in advance and ship everything to your destination. If you don't want to deal with flowers but hate the idea of fake flowers, brooch and button bouquets are trendy and also fit the same DIY-easy bill. Do not forget to bring the glue gun for repairs upon arrival. We've had to fix every single brooch bouquet a client has ever used at one of our weddings. Use lots and lots of bubble wrap when you ship them. And don't plan to toss it, because you'll knock somebody out.

Brooch bouquets have become a wildly popular alternative to fresh or silk flowers. But they have to be packaged carefully for their trip to your destination. (Photo by EP Anderson Photography)

Bride Danyz made silk bouquets for herself and her bridesmaids and shipped them to her destination ahead of her wedding. They were used for additional décor on the cake table after the ceremony. (Photos by EP Anderson Photography)

CHAPTER 9

ཙ ྃ ༀ

MANAGING HELPFUL FRIENDS AND PARENTS—SO THAT YOU CAN PLAN YOUR WEDDING BUT STILL GET THEIR HELP WITH THE DIRTY WORK

Once you've selected your vendors, DIY brides and grooms must figure out what other things they have to do on their own for their wedding. Just because you choose to DIY doesn't mean you have to do *everything* yourselves. It just means you're planning it without a professional planner handling all of the details and keeping your trains running on time on the wedding day. It doesn't mean you can't hire a professional florist at the destination to deliver completed bouquets and centerpieces, or that you have to bake your own wedding cupcakes. You can do that if you want to, but it makes for a pretty un-fun actual wedding week. Take some of the money you saved by not hiring a planner and hire professional vendors to deliver completed services as much as possible.

Regardless of how much you contract out, there will still be a *lot* of things you have to do once you've arrived at your destination, and you need a team of people to help you do it. You can't hire out for most of the dirty work. If you wanted a team of grunts, you'd have hired a wedding planner who brought her own. So you have to warn the people who will be helping construct and execute your actual wedding if you expect them to help.

Remember, it was your brilliant idea to Do It Yourself, right? Okay, so that means that you and your future spouse are doing the hard work and the heavy lifting, not your parents. If you *want* your mom to be intimately involved in your planning, go for it. If you do not want her opinion and you don't let her play with you when you're planning, you cannot expect her to help decorate tables on the big day. It doesn't work that way. Same goes for your girlfriends and buddies who are attending.

If you've chosen to DIY your wedding at a private home or villa, *somebody* has to deal with the rental equipment (maybe even tents), hanging lights, decorating, and general setting up that goes on before a wedding. Hopefully, the caterer will set the tables depending on what you hired him to do, but that's about it. DIYing your wedding means that you have to marshal the troops in advance and make sure they know what exactly you need their help with and when. If the boys are out drinking til the wee hours the night before your wedding, it may be hard to get them out of bed to move the pool table off the porch that needs to be set up as your dinner seating area early the next morning.

Manpower is an oft-forgotten thing by brides and grooms, and it's frankly one of the hardest parts of being a professional wedding planner too, because it's hard to find reliable staffing in remote destinations. Even my planning staff can only do so much of it. If you're going to do it yourselves, you have to realize *there are some things you cannot do by yourself.* Essentially, you've signed up your friends and family as your work crew. Make sure they know this and are on board. Or start bribing them early.

Paula and Buddy's wedding arch, decorated with handprints that represented each of the children they were blending in their two families, was the centerpiece of their gorgeous beach ceremony. But don't underestimate the time it took to create this masterpiece. Even though it's essentially an arts and crafts project until the final assembly, it took literally hours (in the breeze) to get all those handprints on fishing line and anchored into the sand. The handwritten touches made it extra personal for the bride and groom, who were surprised by the arch their children had designed and helped create. (Photos by Mila Orjana)

There is an etiquette to enlisting the help of wedding guests in making your DIY destination wedding happen. You can't invite people as guests without warning them if you plan to have them spend your wedding day stringing lights or setting up your bar. You can't let somebody spend a couple thousand dollars on travel and accommodations and then ask them to be your bartender or photographer at the wedding. Getting them a nice thank-you gift doesn't cut it. When you ask somebody to "work" at your wedding, you need to be clear from the get-go that you are asking for (and will be counting on) their time and attention. They can't be off skiing or basking on a beach if you have them scheduled on your work crew. If you ask somebody to help and they don't want to or make some excuses, let it go and take them off your assignment list. Just because you decided to DIY doesn't mean they signed up for that work detail. Don't be snarky or rude about it; just thank them for being able to be at your wedding and move on. This includes your immediate family members.

Learn from My Experience

Our inaugural year in business, my first few couples with big guest lists wanted to have their friends and family be the setup and tear-down crew for their weddings to save money. That was just fine with me, because it wasn't like I had a big staff of people to call on for all these crazy details the girls wanted, and I would have needed the six to ten guys that I bring with me to every setup now. Back then, I would have panicked.

Unfortunately, that "free labor" concept doesn't usually work very well at destination weddings, because your guests didn't fly thousands of miles to sweat their asses off to make sure your wed-

It's easy to bring the beach theme indoors with something as simple as elegantly labeled starfish as your place cards. (Photo by Saul Padua Photography)

ding chairs are set up, tiki torches mounted, chuppah constructed, lights hung, décor set up, place cards displayed in alphabetical order, etcetera etcetera etcetera—all on a tight deadline, of course. They came for your wedding and to have a vacation.

You have to start setting up your wedding venue early on the wedding day—like eight o'clock in the morning at the latest if you're getting married before it's pitch black outside—and it's not easy to organize a group of young, hung-over adults in someplace like the Caribbean at that hour of the morning.

When we let clients use their friends as crew, half of them didn't show up. The half that did were already partaking of the hair of the dog that bit them the night before, so we ended up with a bunch of half-wasted guys on ladders attempting to string lights by noon. They all got sunburn. They all got grumpy. They didn't follow instructions well because they didn't "get it" that we were following the bride's plan and not just slinging things up in the most expedient way possible.

If you think getting "volunteers" to show up for setup was tough, don't even talk to me about the teardown and cleanup the

It takes longer than you can imagine to build, light, and string all the lanterns used to decorate the atrium of this boutique hotel for the wedding reception. But check out how amazing it looks at night! It's well worth the effort and something you can do with volunteers that doesn't require practice. (Photo by Morris Malakoff)

next day. Very few bother to come back and help. The exceptions to the rule were terrific groups who really had their shit together—in one case, the guys had already taken down the lights and neatly coiled them before I arrived at the agreed-upon ten o'clock the next morning, because they wanted to get it finished so they could go to the beach. Bravo! But they were the exception, not the rule. In more than one case, when I had to initiate wake-up calls to guys sleeping at the venue, I got yelled at by mean, nasty, tired, hungover people who weren't really mad at me. It's not my fault the bride and groom didn't tell you that you were on the work crew.

For these reasons and more, we don't rely on family and friends for the setup and cleanup anymore. Our insurance company won't permit it either, for obvious reasons. But back in the beginning, a lot of what I orchestrated could have been considered DIY.

Involving Your Friends and Family "Just Enough"

You may have chosen to DIY your wedding because you wanted all your sisters and BFFs to help with the planning, or you might be a control freak who doesn't trust anybody else. You have to figure out how much actual involvement you want to give your closest friends and family members before you start the planning. If you don't want anybody's ideas or input, but you expect them to sweat for you at your destination during the wedding weekend, you might have a problem.

Simply put, you cannot blow off your mom, not listen to any of her ideas, and never let her do the fun parts of planning with you (like dress shopping or tasting candy for your dessert bar), but expect her to play slave the weekend of your wedding. Sure, she can take on some of the smaller tasks if she volunteers to do them (like steaming out your wedding gown, for example), but if you have cut her out of your DIY planning, you can't make her do the dirty work when she arrives at the destination. Because I had to fire a bad planner for my own wedding, my mom got stuck helping with a lot more than she'd volunteered for or agreed to do. She and my godmother were excellent sports and saved my butt creating my wedding programs at the last minute (I'd brought the special scallop shell stamp with gold ink that matched my theme, because I'd run out of time at home), they dealt with my gown and veil, and they spent an entire day of what was supposed to be their vacation shipping things home to me after I had left on my honeymoon. For these and many other things, I'm eternally grateful to my mom and her dearest friend, Nan Chandler. But that wasn't how it was supposed to be. And I know for a fact that not everybody's mom is willing to step up to the plate like my mother was. I was a total nightmare on my wedding week, so she must have had the patience of a saint.

Sometimes Bribery Is Okay

Figure out what you actually need help with and then have a conversation with the main parties involved. This may involve a little bribery and a lot of alcohol in some cases, but you DIYers gotta do what you gotta do.

It's hard for the groomsmen to say "no" to their buddy's request for help after they've just been his guest at a baseball game. Asking your girls for help over a wine tasting you've orchestrated, or just during a super fun girls' night, goes over a lot better than an email listing your expectations of your wedding party. Any edicts like that go over like a lead balloon, and I'd personally suggest avoiding them. The money you spend to impart your appreciation to your friends and siblings should be considered an investment in your wedding, and it's not avoidable. Unless, of course, you want everybody snarking behind your back about how they spent two thousand bucks to get to your wedding and then you made them work their asses off.

Parents have to be approached differently, especially if they're helping with your wedding expenses or picking up most of the tab. You can't expect them to pay the bills but not have any input, and then arrive and get stuck doing a lot of the wedding coordination for you. Just like your friends and siblings, you have to talk to your parents and see what role they want in the DIY process.

Choosing a Specific Person to Run Your Wedding Day

Although I asked for some help, I didn't give up the reins on my wedding day. I wish I had. I didn't have much fun being the bride and the wedding planner. Trust me, during those last few hours when my soon-to-be husband was out to lunch with his groomsmen, I was having a panic attack because the rental chairs hadn't arrived, there were no wine glasses on the tables, and the florist delivered bouquets for me and my bridesmaids that were the exact opposite of what I had ordered. I should have been having fun getting gorgeous with my girlfriends, but all of the issues that cropped up had to be resolved by me.

There was nobody to step in for me and yell at the florist and get things fixed, because I was the only one who knew what was supposed to have been delivered. The chairs finally arrived late and, if I recall correctly, my mom might have set them up with her friends. I went down the aisle thirty-five minutes late because there was nobody to keep me and my six bridesmaids on schedule. Really, you do need somebody with a watch that's keeping all your trains running on time that day, including the wedding party.

You have to be prepared to turn over all your schedules, orders, contracts, and telephone numbers for vendors over to that *one particular person* whom you really trust to follow all of your instructions and to troubleshoot where necessary. If the cake is not exactly as ordered, they'll handle it if it's fixable. If the rental equipment isn't delivered on time, they're demon-dialing the rental company until somebody finally responds. This is the role that many wedding planners will try to get you to hire them for— the Day-Of Coordinator. Don't waste the money. Unless you don't have anybody you can count on coming to your wedding, a professional day-of planner isn't going to be any more help than a bossy, meticulous cousin.

Because that professional day-of planner hasn't booked your vendors, negotiated your contracts, or actually planned your wedding, if something goes wrong, there's a *huge* chance that you're going to find yourself totally and completely screwed. She won't necessarily have any backup vendors she can call in at the last minute, and she's got no weight or leverage to use on the vendors. She's just a name to them, and not even the one on the contract. When something goes wrong and you look at her to fix it, she's going to shrug and say you didn't hire her to plan your wedding. You hired her to execute the plan you created with the vendors you selected. If they screw it up, she's going to fix what she can— which isn't much—and not accept responsibility for anything that wasn't in her contract. Do not imagine a day-of coordinator to be your fairy godmother, because she doesn't think of you that way. You're just a one-day client who didn't organize your wedding very well if everything starts falling apart.

So with that said, you are far better off choosing your most detail-oriented friend or family member to play this role. It cannot be somebody in the wedding party, because she can't be sending girls down the aisle if she's part of the lineup walking. She can't make sure your appetizers are coming out of the kitchen to your guests during cocktail hour while you're off taking formal photos if she's part of the crew in the pictures. This person can only have one responsibility that day, and that job is to make sure your wedding is executed as seamlessly as possible, given the information you've provided her beforehand.

Hand Out "Volunteer" Schedules Ahead of Your Wedding Week

Just because your friends all promised to help a year ago when you first decided to DIY your wedding doesn't mean they remember that commitment when the time finally comes. It's a good idea to gently begin reminding everybody about a month ahead of time. This can be another opportunity to do something nice for your wedding party as a pre-wedding thank-you for all the hard work they're going to do to help you execute a flawless DIY wedding.

It's a good idea to give your friends a schedule that tells them *exactly* when they will be needed on site at the wedding venue for the setup and teardown responsibilities they've been assigned ahead of time. That way, the ones who are married can warn their spouses if they're abandoning them for the day, and nobody acts surprised when they find out they're climbing ladders instead of hanging out on the beach.

Make it as fun as possible. If you're expecting the crew to help all day, arrange for lunch to be delivered midway through. Make sure you have coolers of icy beverages on hand for them to grab without having to hunt. Provide all the supplies they'll need—don't expect them to find ladders and extension cords and other things that aren't usually provided at a rental house. Unless your venue specifically says they have something, assume they don't. Find out where to buy it (in advance) as soon as you arrive, or plan to ship everything from the double-sided tape to the power strips.

CHAPTER 10

ುದ್ದ

FINDING A MINISTER AND UNDERSTANDING THE MARRIAGE LICENSE REQUIREMENTS

The most popular trend in wedding ceremonies right now is to have a friend or family member perform your actual ceremony. This trend actually began twenty years ago when Joey married Monica and Chandler on *Friends* by registering himself as a minister online. I honestly think it was the first time most people realized that could even be done. It can be, and quite easily in most places in the continental United States.

However, many states and many places outside the States require that the ministers actually be registered (and in some cases licensed and permitted, having registered and paid fees to the local government). The rules are different in different places—and you cannot trust the information on the Internet. There are usually some ordained online ministers at attractive wedding destinations, and you'll be able to find somebody's name through online research. But you have to make sure you've got *all* the paperwork requirements down pat because they change, quite regularly, in some places.

Puerto Rico has a relatively easy marriage license process, but you wouldn't believe that if you looked it up on the Internet and tried to figure it out yourself. The rules change constantly, but the informational websites do not. Some of the government sites are going to be accurate, but if you're not searching for the information in Spanish, you're not going to find it written down clearly, concisely, and correctly *anywhere* by looking it up on your own. You really, truly need a person on the ground at your destination to review the list of requirements with you. The rules change all the time—I'm not exaggerating about this—and what was true in a posting you found last month may be completely out of date when you get married. Nothing in the world freaks out a DIY bride and groom more than arriving at the marriage license office at their destination to find out they do not, in fact, have the right paperwork.

Just as an example, let me tell you how much things have changed in Puerto Rico in the more than eight years I've been here planning weddings. Initially, brides and grooms had to bring lab reports from venereal disease tests with a letter from their doctor, and then buy a $20 stamp for the license. Then they did away with the lab work for non-residents of Puerto Rico and just required a doctor's letter saying you didn't have anything funky. Suddenly, they added an affidavit of residency requirement, whereby you have to prove you're not a citizen of Puerto Rico in order to skip the sexually transmitted disease tests. Then, copies of birth certificates were needed to get the paperwork for the wedding. Then one day they told me the price of the stamps for "destination wedding" brides and groom had increased from $20 to $150—literally overnight. Seriously. I'm on the ground here and in and out of the demographic office on a weekly basis, and still I find these things out when I arrive and don't have all my ducks in a row. Imagine how hard it is for a DIY couple going off random, probably outdated, information on the web.

Get All Marriage License Requirements Confirmed a Month Ahead of Your Wedding

DIYers using a local wedding officiant should have received, as part of the contracted package, instructions on the paperwork process, and you should confirm those details with the minister before your wedding week. Don't assume they remembered to tell you about some new change.

My clients get *red alert* email messages from me with any changes as soon as I find out about them, but even so, upon their arrival on the island, I still check, double-check, and triple-check everything with each and every client to avoid problems upon arrival. And even then, some of my clients will screw it up—even though they have it in writing from me—and suddenly we have to find a notary because they didn't get their residency affidavit within the time window permitted. Fortunately for my clients, I know how to fix the problem. But if you are a DIY couple with no hookups, finding a doctor to sign a letter or a lawyer to stamp your affidavit (in some places, only attorneys can be notaries), in the midst of delivering your welcome bags, prepping your events, and greeting your guests as they arrive at your destination is a seriously big problem.

Having a Friend Act as Your Wedding Officiant

First, remember that you can always have a friend marry you at your destination and then get married by a justice of the peace back at home. That's the easiest way to handle this part of your wedding if you're getting married someplace remote or complicated and you don't have a wedding planner.

You can also have your friend get ordained online through a number of different "churches" and then have them officially marry you back home where the paperwork is indubitably easier and less expensive to complete than it will be in your destination. The actual online ordination shouldn't cost more than $39.99 unless your friend wants to be silly and order fancy fake licenses and a parking placard that declares him or her to be a "Minister." It's unlikely you'll be able to be married legally at a remote or international destination by this person unless he or she fulfills all the local jurisdiction's requirements, but there's no rule that says you have to get legally married at your destination. You can complete all the paperwork back home, though it won't say you got married at your destination. It will say you got married wherever you got the marriage license. Nobody needs to know what your marriage license says except you, your fiancé, the minister, and your witnesses. Let everybody think you sealed the deal at the destination. It's none of their business anyway.

CHAPTER 11

❧❦

WRITING YOUR WEDDING CEREMONY AND WHY YOU SHOULD GET IT OVER WITH IMMEDIATELY

One of my favorite scenes in my TLC reality show "Wedding Island" was in the second episode, when a really difficult bride named Jessica was actually writing her wedding vows *after* the time she was supposed to go down the aisle. No, I'm not joking. If you saw the show, you were dying along with me at the closed captions as she searched the Internet for her wedding "vowels." That's what she called them, over and over again. "Wedding vowels." Special, huh? And she wasn't kidding. She didn't know the difference.

What was not funny was that after me badgering them for the ceremony plan for weeks, the groom handed me a disheveled stack of papers—partially handwritten—and had me give them to the minister as they headed down the aisle, thirty minutes late, with the final request: *"Can he do it in Spanish?"* Really?

Um, the ceremony is written in English. Yeah, the officiant's bilingual, but it's super hard for anybody to translate on the fly and make it sound smooth. Rev. Franco pulled it off because he's the man, but you can't expect just any wedding officiant to be able to roll with it like that—especially if this isn't what they do every weekend (and in more than one language).

Prepping Your Minister

A professional destination-wedding officiant will probably provide a ceremony planning guide to help you put together the ceremony you want them to perform. If not, you can find samples and examples of other couples' wedding ceremonies online and steal the format from them. Just create a nice, clean Word document to send to the minister so they can space it out the way they prefer and make any notes and ask you questions ahead of time.

Even if your friend who is officiating is the funniest guy in the world and known to be an excellent public speaker, you cannot put the burden of planning your wedding in his hands. You must create the wedding ceremony, choose your vows, select the words you'll use when you exchange rings, and tell him how you want to be introduced as man and wife. Leave blanks for your friend to insert a "homily" of sorts about you two, but this should be a brief interlude where he talks about you and your future lives together, not a recitation of his history with you or your résumés. Believe me, we've heard it all.

Creativity is one thing—I've seen some hilarious improvisations by guest ministers, including one who held the ceremony paperwork inside a *People* magazine so that its cover was what faced the wedding guests. I wouldn't want that at my wedding, but the bride and groom thought it was hilarious, and so did all of their guests. I've seen the *Princess Bride* lines used about ten times, so don't think you're being original, and only use them if they have a real significance to the two of you, because half of your guests won't know what's going on.

However you choose to exchange your vows, swap rings, and make your promises, only you and your fiancé can determine exactly how those things should be worded. And you should write the wedding ceremony very early in your planning to get it over and done with, because it's one of the most commonly procrastinated items in wedding planning. Don't be that couple who is up all night writing vows instead of getting beauty sleep before their wedding. You'll look like hell in your wedding pictures.

CHAPTER 12

❧❧❦

HOW TO HANDLE YOUR VENDORS
AT YOUR DESTINATION WHILE PLANNING
AND EXECUTING YOUR WEDDING

Bridezillas do not fare well in remote biospheres where everybody talks to everybody else. If you're bitchy to one vendor, the whole town will be trash-talking you even before you've called the rest of the folks you need to hire. I explained the cultural differences you need to be attuned to in Chapter 8. That wasn't an exaggeration.

Kid gloves are *always* required when you're thousands of miles away and do not have an advocate working on your behalf there. Even when you make your advance trip to visit (and you should, although some of you will go in blind on your wedding week), you need to be sweet and nice to everyone and keep your opinions about what you've seen and heard to yourselves. You never know which vendors will have to work together in order to make your wedding come off—do not risk giving the power of destruction to somebody you decided not to hire. It's not worth it.

The Rumor Mill or, As We Call It, the Coconut Grapevine

You will probably interview a lot of vendors that you won't end up hiring for any variety of reasons. Maybe you didn't love the menus they sent you, their references didn't check out completely, or you just got a funky vibe when you did your consultation. Whatever reason you had for not choosing them was probably good. With that said, you should be polite to everyone, even the people you do not hire.

After a consultation, and especially after a vendor has provided a bid, you have to give them the courtesy of a notification if you're not going to hire them as soon as you've made that decision. A polite emailed note saying something like "Thank you for your time. We've decided to go another direction," is totally sufficient. You absolutely, positively should not tell them *why* you decided not to hire them. They will be offended, no matter how professional you intend your message to sound. Nobody in the whole world likes to be told they're not "good enough."

The Unintended Consequences of Upsetting a Vendor You're Not Hiring

As you can imagine, most destination wedding locations are fairly small communities. In tourist towns, the vast majority of people have more than one job. Everybody knows everybody else, and because there's nothing else to do on a slow off-season night, they will make jokes and gossip about ridiculous requests from potential brides and grooms from their barstool with anybody who will listen.

If the story about you is horrendous, it could be enough to flag you with every wedding vendor you've yet to hire. I know of several occasions where vendors hiked up prices because brides were "bitchy" or grooms were "assholes" when requesting and negotiating bids. You might not think you've done anything wrong—especially if you're an attorney who is used to getting his or her own way with sharp words—but you are so very wrong. Emails from nasty potential clients get shared and ridiculed.

Another concern should center around the fact that many vendors have to work together for larger events in smaller destinations. What exactly do I mean by that? I mean that if you're having a big wedding and you need the caterer to serve one hundred guests, it's highly likely that a small caterer will ask a colleague at the destination to loan or rent him some of the things he needs to complete your service. Extra silverware, dishes, wine glasses, champagne flutes, and passing trays, just to name a few things, might be on your caterer's list of things he needs to borrow. If you already hurt the feelings of the caterer whom he's asking for help, it's very, very unlikely that other caterer will come to his aid. The other caterer will conveniently have their own event (even if they don't) that night so there's nothing spare to loan out. Yikes! I'm certain you never thought of that. I wouldn't have if I hadn't seen it in action.

Keep Your Opinions about Other Vendors to Yourself

Just because you think you've bonded with the chef you selected doesn't mean you should trash the ones you rejected and figure you have total immunity. Wedding vendors don't have confidentiality clauses (although maybe some of us should), and we have no obligation not to share what we know with anybody we feel like telling. Most of my vendors are friends with each other despite the fact they are business competitors.

I remember when I picked up an emergency "unfuck my wedding" client six weeks before the wedding. They'd called me months before, but when I wouldn't negotiate my fee, they decided to DIY their wedding. It did not go well for them. When they contacted me six weeks out during a heavy wedding season, my initial response was "too late." Then the bride called crying, so I ended up tacking on a *huge* last-minute fee to make all the extra work worth my while. Essentially, they spent almost twice as much for my services as they would have if they'd only hired me to plan it from the beginning. The truth is it takes more time to unfuck a wedding and re-plan everything than it does to start from scratch.

Less than twenty-four hours into the planning, I'd heard every unbelievable thing imaginable from the other vendors they'd contacted (half of whom weren't going to work with them or hadn't completed their contracts with the couple and didn't intend to do so before I stepped in). The best screw-up was the rehearsal dinner planned for a restaurant's top deck that could hold a maximum of thirty-five guests. My clients had more than one hundred and fifty people attending. One of the caterers who'd stopped returning their calls made a huge joke about it when she found out I had taken over the planning and was moving the rehearsal dinner to another location.

"Damn," she said. "I'll have to make other plans for that day. We were all planning to bring coolers and set up beach chairs across the street and see how long til the whole place collapsed." She was joking, but she wasn't kidding. I've made jokes likes that about venues to some of my vendors in the past, because safety really is a serious issue and it's not something everyone thinks about. DIY brides and grooms don't have any idea how many guests a space can actually hold. And if you're at a remote destination where the chances of a visit from the Fire Marshal are nil, vendors desperate for your money may not be candid about their actual safe capacity.

In fact, the owners of this particular establishment had not informed the clients of the maximum capacity of the venue and they hadn't planned to do so. They were going to have that party upstairs and just keep their fingers crossed. It was a flat-out dangerous situation and the first thing I cancelled when I took over the wedding. But back to my original point—all the wedding vendors on the island knew about this couple and absolutely *hated them*. I had to pull some serious favors to get them the things they needed to complete their wedding planning. The acoustic guitar trio would only agree to play their ceremony music if they didn't have to speak to either the bride or groom. I wouldn't normally agree to that, but these were extenuating circumstances.

Having your reputation as "clients from hell" across the island before your wedding is planned is a big, hot mess in the making. You can't do anything that would make that happen. No matter what you think of a vendor or her services, keep those thoughts to yourselves and just hire the vendors you do like.

There Are Ears Everywhere at Your Destination

When you visit your destination to plan your wedding, and especially once you're there for your wedding, be careful what you say to people and how you treat the servers and bartenders in the establishments you visit.

As I mentioned in Chapter 8, you never know when you're going to come across the same people who served you lunch mixing cocktails at your wedding reception. A particularly bad bartender could be an absolutely amazing photographer. Finding out you screwed your wedding photographer on her tip the night before, when she was your bartender, can be a nasty reality check if you don't find out who she is until she arrives with her camera gear to shoot your dressing photos.

CHAPTER 13

ℰℭ

START WRITING YOUR WEDDING SCHEDULE AS SOON AS YOU START DEALING WITH THE VENDORS

*M*ost experienced wedding vendors will tell you how much time they need for setup, or if they need earlier access to the venue than normal to make deliveries. But if they don't, a DIY bride needs to ask all of these questions in the very beginning and start sketching out a solid wedding schedule from day one.

Scheduling the little details from the get-go will help you to realize that, if you were lucky enough to find a company that would come do your lighting and décor setup, you'll need the rental equipment delivered and set up much earlier, because you cannot light a tent that hasn't arrived to be set up. Make sure you time the cake's arrival depending on what climate you're in and what kind of frosting you've chosen. It's not rocket science, but it needs to all go onto the same document in an hour-by-hour format (or, in some cases, minute-by-minute format) for every day of your wedding events, starting with the welcome bag delivery.

Here's an example of what a wedding schedule might look like, although you'll certainly fill in all your own details based on what kind of vendors you're using and where you're getting married. Be sure to include specific directions and location names for everything, unless it's the only hotel in town. Then you can just write "hotel." This sample schedule is based loosely on my own wedding plan back in 2004, and the only thing I've changed in more than eight years of planning is the level of detail included. My professional schedules are considerably more comprehensive.

Monday

4:00 p.m.   Bride and groom arrive at destination and pick up rental car (or are picked up by shuttle or whatever the plan is).

5:00 p.m.   Bride and groom check into wedding venue—coordinate check-in time with property managers/hotel desk in advance.

6:00 p.m.   Quick shopping trip to get snacks and drinks to keep in the room.

7:00 p.m.   Unpack boxes and begin stuffing welcome bags (we'd shipped down thirty-two boxes via UPS that were all waiting in our room).

8:30 p.m.   Go to dinner (make reservations in advance so that you actually get out and go—you may be feeling overwhelmed and exhausted, but you need to take care of yourselves and have some alone time away from the mess and to-do lists).

11:00 p.m. Finish stuffing welcome bags before bed.

Tuesday

8:00 a.m.   Go to the demographic office to do marriage license paperwork (this will vary based on where you're getting married and how their process works).

Noon   Deliver welcome bags to guests staying someplace other than our venue.

2:00 p.m.   Meet with caterer to confirm details.

3:00 p.m.   Meet with florist to confirm details.

4:00 p.m.   Meet with hairdresser for practice beauty run (and don't be afraid to speak up if you hate it or you'll end up looking like I did, with J. Lo hair and too much makeup).

7:00 p.m.   Last dinner alone (again, make reservation in advance someplace nice).

9:00 p.m.   Back in room—finish making ceremony programs (a project my mom and godmother got stuck finishing for us because we ran out of time) and burning CDs for during the band breaks (should have been done weeks before).

Wednesday

8:00 a.m.   Back to the demographic office to pick up the marriage license paperwork we'd filed for the previous day.

10:00 a.m. Finish delivering welcome bags (not every private villa is easy to access, and you have to make arrangements in advance with caretakers and property managers based on when the previous guests checked out).

Noon   Wedding guests begin arriving on the island. Be at the hotel to greet them.

3:00 p.m.   Take guests who have arrived for a swim at Green Beach.

Evening   Informal—everybody on their own for dinner.

Thursday

10:00 a.m. Call all vendors (and visit those who don't answer) to confirm times again.

Noon   Remainder of guests arrive on the island and get settled in their accommodations.

6:00 p.m.   Welcome party at bar along the water on the Malecón.

Late night Hang out at hotel (which works great unless your younger guests are going to keep your older guests up all night—I heard a *lot* of complaining on Friday morning).

Friday

9:00 a.m.   Breakfast for the wedding party at the hotel.

10:00 a.m. Wedding rehearsal (with cocktails) on the terrace of the hotel—*wedding party and immediate family only, please!*

Noon– Beach party pig roast with bottomless sangria at Red Beach
5:00 p.m. (A lot of fun but entirely too much alcohol in the sun for most of my guests. I'd recommend limiting the beach party to three hours max).

7:00 p.m. Biobay tours (we treated our group to a tour of the island's famous bioluminescent bay—fortunately, they didn't breathalyze anybody before we got onto the boat).

9:00 p.m. Rehearsal dinner at Tradewinds Restaurant.

11:30 p.m. Bride in bed (except it didn't work out that way and it was after three a.m. when four other bridesmaids dragged one passed-out member of my bridal party out of my room).

11:30 p.m. Groom to sleep in another room (remember to figure out where you're putting him in advance, because our plan fell to shit when two of my guests hooked up in the room where Bill was supposed to be crashing).

Saturday—The Wedding Day

9:00 a.m. Breakfast delivered to the bride in her room (so I wouldn't see my groom).

9:30 a.m. Groomsmen breakfast. Groom gives wedding party gifts to the guys.

10:00 a.m. Decorating crew goes to reception venue to hang lights and set up place cards and favors.

10:00 a.m. Massage for the bride (a treat from my mom that I didn't enjoy because I was way too uptight and just wanted to be moving around and getting things done—DIY brides don't really have the luxury of unnecessary spa treatments on the big day).

11:00 a.m. Caterer arrives to set up bridesmaids' luncheon on the patio.

Noon Bridesmaids' luncheon on the patio outside the bridal suite. Give gifts to the bridal party.

1:00 p.m.   Beauty team arrives to do hair and makeup for the bride and the bridal party (we didn't leave nearly enough time on my wedding day—you need to solidly block forty-five minutes per bridesmaid for hair and makeup each, and twice as long for a picky bride. Plus forty-five minutes for each mani or pedi, plus drying time).

2:00 p.m.   Rental chairs delivered to the hotel for setup on the terrace (don't forget to assign somebody to do the setup, because the bride is indisposed by this point).

3:30 p.m.   Photographer begins dressing photos with the bride (be sure you have something appropriate to wear) while she's having her hair and makeup done.

This bride had comfy clothes to wear while she was getting gorgeous and then slipped into a white silk kimono for the final moments. (Photo by Saul Padua)

Her gown hung waiting for her in a bridal suite they'd decorated with leftover décor from her bridal shower, like the flags. (Photo by Saul Padua)

3:30 p.m.   Wedding cake is delivered to reception venue by the cake lady.

4:00 p.m.   Florist delivers bridal party flowers to the hotel (the wrong flowers, in my case).

4:15 p.m.   Musician arrives for ceremony music setup.

4:30 p.m.   Florist delivers centerpieces and décor to the reception venue (make sure you have somebody there to confirm that everything was delivered and actually gets placed where you intended it).

Some couples have a very explicit setup in mind when they create their décor. You have to provide an exact chart of how you want things set up or they may not look like what you had in mind. This couple had monogrammed napkins that had to be folded in a certain way, with a special rock placed on top of the napkin. Under the napkins, there was a card explaining the meaning of the rocks. The table numbers and place cards were all backed with maps that reflected the journey in their relationship and places they'd been together. (Photos by Morris Malakoff)

4:30 p.m.   Prelude music begins as guests start arriving for the ceremony.

4:30 p.m.   Groom and groomsmen dressed and ready to receive guests at the ceremony.

4:45 p.m.   Wedding officiant arrives to perform the ceremony.

4:55 p.m.   Ask guests to be seated after you confirm bridal party is ready to go down the aisle. At most destination weddings, they'll be wandering around taking pictures of themselves at your fabulous venue with amazing views until go-time.

5:00 p.m.   Wedding ceremony (okay, truthfully, I went down the aisle late at 5:35 pm).

6:00 p.m.   Wedding cocktail reception begins at reception venue while pictures are being taken of wedding party back at ceremony site.

6:00 p.m.   Band arrives for setup in the dining room at the reception.

6:45 p.m.   Bride and groom make their grand entrance (You can have somebody announce you with a phrase like, *"Ladies and Gentlemen, for the first time ever, appearing as a married couple, Mr. and Mrs. Bill and Sandy Malone"*).

7:00 p.m.   Guests move from cocktail area to dining room and are seated for dinner—blessing is asked by person of your choosing (pre-designate this person so they're prepared—and don't do it at all if it makes you uncomfortable).

7:00 p.m.   Band begins playing during dinner.

8:00 p.m.   Toasts—after dinner plates have been cleared and beverages have been refreshed (or champagne poured).
Best Man
Maid of Honor
Parents of the Bride
Bride and Groom toast and thank their guests (you can do whatever you like, that's just the most traditional way to handle it—if you didn't have a formal rehearsal dinner with toasts, you slide the groom's parents right in there before the bride's).

8:20 p.m.   First dance
Father/daughter dance

Mother/son dance

Any other special family dances (get it all over with at once so you don't have to keep stopping the party later on).

8:30 p.m.   Dance and party music

9:30 p.m.   Cut the cake

10:30 p.m. Toss the bouquet/garter

11:00 p.m. Reception finished—cleanup team packs up leftover favors, decorations, and takes down whatever décor must be removed that night (of course, this only works if your teardown crew is sober and hasn't taken off to the nearest bar).

11:30 p.m. Tip your vendors before you leave your venue (and be sure to note who you didn't get to tip so you can do it first thing the next day, i.e., cake lady, florist).

Pack for honeymoon before going to bed.

Sunday

10:00 a.m. Farewell breakfast with the guests at the hotel.

11:00 a.m. Cleanup crew returns to the venue to finish cleanup not completed the night before (if you can find them to get them to help).

Noon   Meet with various vendors to settle bills and pay tips.

2:00 p.m.   Bride and groom depart island for honeymoon (leaving Mother of the Bride to deal with shipping back all the ridiculous stuff the DIY bride sent down for the wedding).

The Importance of the Detailed Schedule

So you've read all that, and now you think I'm crazy. My husband jokes that the only schedule more detailed than what I write for a wedding is the itinerary of the US Secret Service on Inauguration Day. And he's not kidding. I believe that knowledge is power and schedules give me control. When I put a schedule on a clipboard and walk into a room, vendors give me a little bit more respect. Every DIY bride should have a few clipboards with her at her destination.

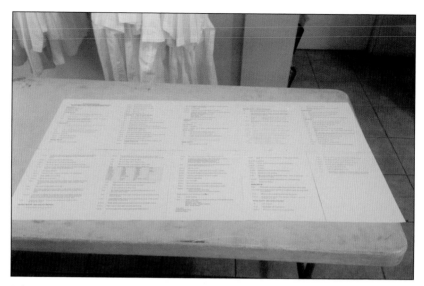

This is a real picture of a professional wedding planner's schedule on a week with more than one wedding. The colors of ink represent the different brides and grooms. Although you'll only have one wedding on your schedule, yours will be just as long and detailed once you've added in all your travel and personal information.

You can start writing your schedule as soon as you start booking your vendors, and then you add to it and tweak it as you go along. It's the best and only way to keep track of everything in a way that makes sense, so that you don't have vendors overlapping or forget anybody important. If they're not on the schedule, you might forget to confirm them, and they might forget about your wedding. Don't try to use fancy software or a spreadsheet—just do a Word document so you can tweak, add, and edit as you see fit. You're going to spend a lot of time working on this schedule.

The Three Kinds of Wedding Schedules
Master Schedule
This is the most important schedule you will write. It has every single detail about everything for your wedding weekend on it. You

should include all your personal travel details and anything else that you need to supervise, confirm, or do during the days leading up to your wedding. The schedule may actually begin, for you, a week prior to arriving at your destination.

Vendor Schedule

The Vendor Schedule is just as important to the vendors as your Master Schedule is to you, but they don't need all that personal information. This schedule should be slimmed down to only include vendor times and information. Take out all of the information about where you are and what you're up to, as well as where your guests are staying and when they're coming and going. Although you might trust your caterer (whom you've only met twice), you have no idea who in his kitchen will see that detailed schedule. It's a blueprint for your wedding and it has too much personal information on it for the whole world to see. In fact, the only time we ever had a burglary problem during a wedding I planned on Vieques was when the wedding party invited some unsavory folks back to their accommodations to "party" and they got their hands on the schedules. The burglars hit a different house every night, exactly when the occupants were elsewhere at a pre-scheduled wedding event. For security reasons, only give your vendors the information they need about the services they're providing for your wedding.

Wedding Party Schedule

The Wedding Party Schedule should be given to every bridesmaid and groomsman, immediate members of the family, and anybody else with a role in the wedding activities. If you've shanghaied more of your friends into being on your setup and teardown work crews, they'll need copies of this schedule as well. It tells everybody where they have to be, when they have to be there, and what they need to bring with them to be prepared. You can share this schedule with your helper friends via email ahead of the wedding, but you should be prepared with printed copies for them when they arrive for your wedding weekend. Most won't bring them. Bring one for everybody who needs it, plus extras.

CHAPTER 14

ഇരു

NEWSLETTERS, WELCOME LETTERS, AND WELCOME BAGS—TIPS FOR A SMOOTH GUEST ARRIVAL

*Y*ou've asked all your nearest and dearest to travel to a destination of your choosing for your wedding day, but not everybody who is attending may be well-traveled or comfortable with the kind of place you've chosen to get married. It's your job to provide them with as much information (ahead of time *and* upon arrival) as possible so that they feel entirely comfortable about the trip. We do this via a two-step process that you can easily adapt for your own destination wedding.

Newsletters

Your guests may have received their travel information packet and invitation months ahead of your wedding, if you planned it well, but as your wedding date nears, you need to give them more detailed information about the schedule for the destination wedding weekend so that they can make their own plans and know exactly how to pack. You can put it in a PDF file format and email it out to all of your guests, and you can also post it on your wedding website. Don't forget to mail it to the people on your list who are not online (older relatives, generally speaking).

The newsletter can be fun and silly, like the example below of what we write for our clients. Or it can be serious and professionally designed. Whatever floats your wedding boat is what you should use, but remember to include the following information:

- A brief outline of the wedding weekend (can be a note from you or a faux news article like we use)
- All of the times and locations for scheduled events
- Information about special activities they may want to book on their own ahead of arrival
- Contact information for you and the groom at the destination in case they run into any problems en route to your wedding

A newsletter doesn't need to include directions or addresses; you'll put that stuff into your welcome letter. The purpose of the newsletter is to save yourself from the deluge of phone calls and emails from guests with questions in the final weeks leading up to your destination wedding departure.

Welcome Bags and Welcome Letters
I strongly urge every DIY wedding couple to take the time and spend the money to do legitimate welcome bags to have waiting for your guests upon their arrival at your destination. If you do it properly, you're going to need a significant amount of space. Beach bags are popular for tropical destination weddings, whereas gift baskets and boxes seem to be more popular for cold weather des-

VIEQUES WEDDING NEWS

Vol. 8, Number 16   Wedding Date: Sat., April 11, 2015

Countdown Begins for Wedding of the Century

Susan Smith
Will Marry Robert Jones
In a Sunset Ceremony
On Vieques Island

Vieques Island, Puerto Rico – Plans are well under way for what has been dubbed "The Wedding of the Century" by locals on the tiny Caribbean island of Vieques, Puerto Rico.

Susan Smith and Robert Jones will exchange vows at Playa Martineau at 5 o'clock in the evening on the 11th of April. The bride will wear a champagne trumpet-style designer gown. Her bridesmaids will wear designer dresses. And everyone is hoping that Mr. Jones and his groomsmen show up wearing at least pants. Guests are also requested to wear at least pants.

Ms. Smith has planned an event-filled weekend including a welcome party, tours of the famous biobay, a beach party, a beach ceremony, and a sunset reception at one of the most beautiful venues on the island.

The winners of the water wing races will be named "Best Man" and "Maid of Honor," regardless of gender. The winner of the gecko races will be the wedding officiant. The iguana-riding competition has been cancelled due to an unfortunate event at the last wedding (no wedding guests were injured). Get well cards can be sent to the iguanas care of the Vieques Humane Society.

SCHEDULE OF EVENTS

Thursday, April 9th

Welcome to Vieques!!!

8-10 pm – Welcome Party
(Duffy's in Esperanza)

Friday, April 10th

12-3 pm – Beach Party
(Playa Sun Bay)

Evening – Tours of the Famous Bioluminescent Bay
Please call now to make your reservations! Tours get booked up!
- Island Adventures (big electric boat) – (787) 741-0720
- Abe's Snorkeling (kayaks) – use code "XXX" to get discounted rate per person (787) 741-2134

Saturday, April 11th

5 pm – Wedding Ceremony and Reception
(Playa Martineau)

If you have any problems en route to Vieques or once you've arrived, please call our wedding planners.
Sandy Malone XXX-XXX-XXXX or Bill Malone XXX-XXX-XXXX from Weddings in Vieques

Some welcome bags feel like "swag bags" from a fancy red carpet event, and others just provide the basic information the guests need. Vanessa and Pablo struck a happy medium with their welcome bags, adding some rum and other snacks to make it complete!

tinations. With that said, nobody takes the basket or box home with them and everybody will bring home a good tote bag and use it, so I think nice bags are worth the investment wherever you're getting married.

You only have to give one welcome bag per couple, and one bag per single guest. If you have several singletons staying together in a room, you have to give a welcome bag to each of them. You can't expect them to share something they can't all take home with them afterwards. Also, you'll find that many of your guests will use the bags throughout your wedding weekend to carry things to your events. They come in very handy.

What to Put in a Wedding Welcome Bag

It is not necessary to spend a fortune on welcome bags as long as you put the critical things inside them. If you get nice, reusable fabric bags (because paper gift bags can't handle the weight of the inserts and will split and cause a big mess when you're delivering them), the bag is a gift itself. I know of many couples who opt to skip giving reception favors and use that money to goose up the welcome bag contents instead.

Before you spend a lot of money on shipping and personalization, check with the nicer shops you visited at your destination and see if anybody has something with a map of the area or name of the town that you like. If you don't need that many bags, this is a more cost-effective way to go and you won't have to ship anything. You can pick them up when you arrive if the shop will hold them for you.

While you have lots of options for things to put inside a destination wedding welcome bag, the following things *must* be included:

- A welcome letter (details to follow on how to write this)

- Local publications with information about your destination
- Flyers and pamphlets highlighting activities and local attractions your guests might want to explore
- Maps (as many different versions as are readily available; some of the cartoony ones in tourist areas are adorable but not so great for navigation)
- Beverages (a couple of bottles of water are sufficient if you don't want to get fancy)
- A snack (doesn't have to be fancy—sometimes bags of pretzels and cookies are more than enough)

You certainly aren't limited to the above list; in fact, I encourage you to put some fun things in there too. But the key is to have that bag—with the information about *where* they need to be, *when* they need to be there, and *how to find* the location—waiting for them when they arrive. Including a drink and something to munch is a good idea if your guests have been traveling all day and will have to venture forth from their accommodations to seek restaurants, or shop for their own goodies. If they're starving when they arrive, they'll be grumpy. You can help reverse that mood by providing something they can easily grab and eat.

Many of my clients get super-creative with their welcome bags—I know I did that too. Some of it I regret because, let's face it, although all the fun stuff we find in the dollar aisle at Target seems like a good idea at the moment when you're buying it, you have to pay to ship all of that to your destination, because you sure won't have room in your luggage. Think lightweight. Think disposable (they may not have room in their luggage either). Here are some of the most common things my clients put into their welcome bags:

- Beer cozies (usually personalized, but the inflatable pink

flamingos are my favorite)
- Gourmet cookie treats (wedding cake or bride and groom cookies, hopefully from a local vendor so they're not hard as rocks by the time your guests receive them)
- Locally-produced products such as honey and hot sauce
- Destination-themed items (it's popular to give local rum, a can of Coke, and bottle of fruit juice in Puerto Rico so guests can make a rum punch or Cuba Libre as soon as they get into their rooms)
- Playing cards (sometimes personalized, but not always)
- Beach towels
- Cheesy sunglasses
- Bug repellent (especially important if you're getting married in the woods)
- Sunscreen (very useful for tropical destinations and ski slopes)

Think carefully before you purchase your welcome bag gifts. I tell all of my clients that "Chapstick, chocolate, candles, and lots of other things that don't begin with the letter C all melt in the Caribbean." Don't mail yourself things to stuff in a welcome bag that are going to arrive melted and disgusting. Use common sense.

You can personalize just about anything in the world now, and I believe we've seen it all. Just keep in mind how much money you're spending on each bag, because it adds up quickly. Be smarter than I was when I DIY'd my wedding. Learn from my mistakes and save yourselves a bundle of money. You do not need to order personally labeled water bottles by the case and pay hundreds of dollars in shipping. Just order the labels and then slap them over the ones on the bottles you buy at the store at your destination. If you want to waste hours soaking off the brand labels, go for it. But that's certainly optional and totally unnecessary.

With the rising cost of checked baggage, many guests will try to carry-on everything. Don't give them items they can't transport in the airplane cabin. Larger bottles of liquids, for example, get abandoned in hotel rooms all the time (not the rum—they always seem to consume that just fine). Personalized corkscrews or anything TSA might determine could be used as a weapon are a no-no too. Keep in mind that you want your guests to consume or be dying to keep everything you put in there that costs you money. When you're DIYing your wedding, you can't afford to waste money on things that are useless to your guests during their trip and will likely be left behind in their hotel rooms.

Writing the Perfect Welcome Letter

If you think you cannot afford to do welcome bags (and that's a really bad idea for destination weddings), you still have to create a welcome packet for your guests with a solid welcome letter, maps, and directions. Without the welcome letter, your guests are literally going to be lost in paradise at your destination, trying to remember where they're supposed to be, and showing up late at everything because they either didn't remember what time the event started or they got lost getting there.

Start with a greeting as an introduction. Tell them you're excited they've arrived. Here's a good example from the letter we use for my clients:

"We hope your trip went well and we're so glad you're here! On Saturday, we'll be taking the biggest step of our lives, and it means so much to us that all of you could be here to share our special day. We have a few hints and tips to help make your stay more enjoyable. Please read through this entire document—it includes some very important information about our wedding weekend that you won't want to miss, including directions to events and the final schedule for the weekend. We can't wait to see you! And welcome to the Caribbean!" Sign it with your names.

We follow the introduction with a list of tips for navigating the island and having a safe and fun trip. Of course, this section of your welcome letter will be personalized to suit your individual destination (if you don't know what you should be writing here, you'd better do some homework so you can give your guests appropriate advice, especially safety tips). Here's an example of what we write in our clients' welcome letters, which is specific to their time on Vieques, of course:

- We've included a map in your welcome bag. *Take it everywhere* with you in case you take a wrong turn and get lost. All of the locations for events on our agenda are shown on the map.
- Drive carefully on the island—especially at night! There are wild horses, cows, iguanas, roosters, and mongoose all over the roads (as if you didn't notice on the way to where you're staying). And wear your seatbelt at all times—there's a hefty fine, and they do enforce it!
- We've included a copy of *Vieques Insider* in your welcome packets. *Vieques Insider* is the monthly newsletter for the island. It has all kinds of useful phone numbers and information in it.
- Wear sunblock and drink a lot of water while you're here. We're much closer to the equator than you're used to, and you'll burn much more quickly here than at any of the beaches up in the United States.
- Vieques is a small, quiet island. It doesn't even have a stoplight. And sometimes that means tourists forget to

use common sense about their general safety like they would at home. Unfortunately, the island isn't quite perfect. Occasionally, there are instances of petty thievery that can really ruin your whole vacation if you don't take the regular precautions you would take when vacationing in any other city. If you make sure to lock the door to your house or hotel room, don't carry enormous amounts of cash, and are aware of your surroundings, you shouldn't have any problems.

- Do not leave anything (even things that aren't valuable) in your rental car when you park it at the beaches. Leave your rental car unlocked. At many of the beaches, you can't see your car from the beach. If somebody wants to rifle through your car, let them. They won't steal it—there's nowhere to go! They can't take a stolen rental car on the ferry off the island. But they will break a window to see what's in a duffle bag left on the back seat. And the rental car company will bill you for the damage.

- There have occasionally been incidences of "banditos" on horseback stealing beach bags and electronics off towels on the beach while tourists were in the water or away on a beach walk. Don't take large amounts of cash to the beach with you. Don't bring credit cards to the beach. Please don't leave anything of value unattended on the beach if you're in an isolated area.

- Don't pick up hitchhikers—unless you know them. And don't hitchhike!

- If you have any problems while you're here, our phone numbers are X and Y. Either one of us can help you if you need assistance (*you can never provide your contact info too many times*).

Seem like too much information to give them? Afraid you're going to scare your guests and make them think you've invited them someplace that isn't safe? Let me tell you right here and right now that most tropical destinations have all of the same problems (and usually more if you're outside the United States), and you would much rather scare your guests into being extra careful than deal with the aftermath of them doing something stupid and having all their identification stolen. Getting the proper paperwork for a guest to fly home can be a nightmare, and if you're a DIY bride and groom, dealing with that will become your problem as soon as it's discovered. Better to warn them early and have them be extra vigilant than to have to apologize because your destination wedding became the worst vacation of their lives. I've never had clients tell me that they wished we hadn't included the safety tips and warnings in the welcome letter.

You should follow up the tips with a final schedule of events, complete with all the details they need so they know when you're going to be feeding them and what they have to schedule on their own. Here's an example of a welcome letter schedule from one of the weddings I planned:

Thursday, June 25th
8–10 p.m. Welcome party at Duffy's in Esperanza! There will be plenty of appetizers and drinks to satisfy!

Friday, June 26th
10 a.m. Wedding rehearsal at the wedding villa—*wedding party and immediate family only, please!*
1–4 p.m. Beach party pig roast at Sun Bay Beach—wear your bathing suits and bring your beach towels and beach chairs! *(Sun Bay is on the Vieques Map—there is a $2/car fee for entry to the beach area—go in and drive up to the water*

and take a left. You'll see us on your right as you proceed down the beach.)

Evening   Tour the famous bioluminescent bay! *If you haven't already made a reservation, call today! Tours book up quickly and this is something you shouldn't miss!* (Here you'd provide information about whatever activity or tour you're recommending, along with contact information for scheduling their tour and any discount codes you've been able to arrange for your wedding group.)

Saturday, June 27th—The Bride and Groom's Big Day!

5:30 p.m.   Wedding ceremony and reception at the villa

After Hours Meet up for dancing and karaoke at a bar (make sure you've let the venue know that you'll be descending on them late at night with a big group)

Be sure to include specific directions to each and every activity featured on the schedule at the end of the welcome letter. There's no such thing as being *too specific* when you're managing a group of wedding guests in an unfamiliar destination. We joke about our job as "herding cats," and so do many of our clients. But it's not as much of a joke to brides and grooms who have to DIY the herding. It's an annoying time-suck during your own wedding weekend.

The end of your welcome letter is the perfect place to provide a list of activities and vendors available at the destination if you don't have a lot of brochures or other information to put into the welcome bag. Depending on where you are, you'll be telling them about skiing, snorkeling, hiking, or sailing vendors, for example. It's also nice to provide information on massage therapists at your destination who will come to them at their accommodations, should they feel the need to spoil themselves.

First Impressions

Your newsletter, and then your welcome bag with its accompanying welcome letter, are the first real impressions you'll give your guests of your DIY destination wedding weekend. You cannot afford to screw them up, and you absolutely, positively cannot get lazy and skip these items. To do so would be really careless of you as DIYers responsible for your guests' comfort and wedding experience. When you decided to DIY, you accepted that you would have to create all these materials yourselves—now do it! Fortunately, you've got great templates to work with from what a professional, experienced destination wedding planner like me uses for her own clients and their guests.

Don't be afraid to get creative with your materials—this is the time to let your DIY-side shine. Pick fun colors of paper and punch holes and tie ribbons to hold them together instead of just slamming in staples. I was desperately afraid my own guests wouldn't read my welcome letters when I got married, so I printed them out on God-awful-bright neon paper, with every page a different color. It was slightly painful to read (or so I was told), but they couldn't claim they hadn't seen the welcome letters in the welcome bags, and they had no excuse if they hadn't actually read them.

CHAPTER 15

⚜

STARTING YOUR PACKING WHEN YOU START YOUR WEDDING PLANNING— THERE'S LITERALLY NO SUCH THING AS TOO EARLY TO BEGIN THAT LIST

*W*hen you DIY your wedding, you're going to start making lists of things that you need to bring with you literally from the first minute you begin making plans. At least, you *should* be writing everything down on lists as soon as you think of the item, lest you forget it later when you're bogged down with writing schedules and confirming your vendors.

Planning Your Wedding Wardrobe
As soon as you know where you're getting married and what events you'll be hosting, you can start to plan your wardrobe for yourself and your fiancé (if your future spouse is anything like my husband, he can't be relied on to prepare in advance and pack on his own, but maybe you are luckier).

Make a list of each and every event that you'll need clothing for—from your trip to your destination to your departure outfit for your honeymoon—and start filling in the blanks with *what exactly* you will each need, including socks, shoes, jewelry, and other accessories. When you start this project, you're going to have a whole lot of blanks to fill because you likely haven't even begun to shop for your outfit to wear to your rehearsal dinner or what cutesy outfit you want to rock as you take off for your honeymoon. The list of what you're going to need (it's okay to just fill in "sundress" or "coat and tie" temporarily) will complete itself as you collect those items in the months prior to your wedding. I strongly recommend you time your wedding wardrobe shopping to coincide with the big sales for the right seasons. We found my husband's designer-label wedding suit at an end-of-summer sale at the outlets and only spent a couple hundred dollars on something that should have cost a thousand.

If you have space in your house for a standing, expandable clothing rack (preferably on wheels), get one! You'll never regret it. They're collapsible, and you can use it for pre-packing in the future, or as a laundry drying rack when the wedding's over if you don't have room for it elsewhere. As you purchase items of clothing specifically for your wedding, go ahead and hang them on the rack, write them into your wardrobe plan, and add them to your packing list. Sometimes it's helpful to put labels on the hanging items so you remember exactly what you were thinking when you bought that particular shirt or skirt.

Using Boxes to Get Organized

My brides and grooms who live in closet-sized apartments in big cities always hate this next piece of advice, but they tell me it's foolproof and worth the frustration every time. Get two clean boxes and put them someplace you won't trip over them. Label one of them "Things to Ship," and label the other one "Things to Pack." A

Bride Shelly opted to wear a beautiful floral hair clip rather than try to keep large flowers anchored in her hair—and alive—throughout her entire Caribbean wedding. (Photo by EP Anderson Photography)

lot of what you'll be buying doesn't go onto a hanger. Shoes, cosmetics, accessories, and even your wedding jewelry should go into one of these designated boxes as soon as it enters your home. You aren't going to wear your wedding lipstick or perfume before the big day, so why should you stash it away someplace you'll have to hunt for it instead of immediately categorizing it in a pre-labeled box? Easy as pie. Anybody who has ever found Christmas gifts they accidentally hid from themselves in July understands exactly what I'm worried about here. The last thing you need to be doing a week before your wedding is scrambling around in a panic looking for the crystal hair pins you bought months ago and put someplace safe so you wouldn't lose them. Yeah, right. We all know that does not work.

Make a Detailed Packing List

Planning your wardrobe out, day by day, is one useful tool for creating your master packing list. But you still have to write a detailed list of everything you need to pack for your clothing needs, all on one page together, including toiletries, cosmetics, and medications. As DIYers, you're going to have a much longer list of things you need to pack and ship, but we'll talk about how to handle all of that in next chapter. Right now, we're talking about making a list of everything you and your fiancé need to pack in order to be clean, dressed, and fabulous at every wedding event you worked so hard to plan.

Don't worry about in what order you write it all down, *just write it down as soon as you think of it.* Deodorant, cufflinks, hand steamer, shoes (by event), passports, cash, hair products, tweezers, contact solution—there's basically nothing you're packing that doesn't belong on this list. I know some of you travel frequently for business and you pack all the time, so you're thinking this is overkill. You are wrong. DIY brides and grooms have so many things to remember to bring for their wedding that it's easy to forget to bring something important like medication or back-up contact lenses for the most important weekend of your life so far. Don't usually wear your glasses? What if you get something in your eye and cannot wear your lenses one day? Pack the spare eyeglasses just in case. If you're getting married someplace sunny, pack at least two pairs of sunglasses for each of you. I guarantee one of you will lose or break at least one pair. Pack the sunscreen too, unless you want to pay tourist prices on the beach or the ski slopes. But you won't remember to buy or pack a lot of these things if they aren't on your master packing list.

Make a Shopping List

You're going to need to buy a whole lot of things that aren't actually clothing, so start a shopping list on a separate page (but don't take those things off your master packing list—it's better to have it there so you don't forget to pack it after you buy it—especially if you ignored my advice about putting things directly into pre-designated boxes).

Don't wait until a month prior to your wedding to buy the easy drugstore stuff that you need. Razor blades, travel-sized bottles, cosmetics, a lint roller, and new tweezers (a must for any bride) can all be purchased as soon as you know you need them. Make the list by store category so you can watch for sales, snag coupons, and pick things up as you run across them during the planning process. You should have *absolutely everything* on your shopping list purchased by sixty days prior to your wedding date. Believe me, if you plan on DIYing your own destination wedding, the last thing you should be struggling with at the two-months-out point is what you're going to wear on your wedding and honeymoon.

Packing for Your Honeymoon

This project should be approached exactly the same way that you're tackling the packing for your destination wedding weekend—way ahead of time! There's no reason you can't start shopping for it as you come across things you'll need and want. First plot your wardrobe, and then make the shopping list. Get things as you come across them. The only thing you might want to wait to buy for your honeymoon is naughty lingerie, because you're probably going to get a ton of that from your friends (and probably your mom) at your bridal shower and bachelorette events.

When you plan your honeymoon packing list, keep in mind that you will both be coming down from an intense wedding weekend. In addition to clothes (and hopefully you won't need too many of those), bring reading material for the both of you and a small speaker you can hook up to your phone wherever you are, so you can listen to your favorite playlists. If you can squeeze a small, soft, collapsible cooler into your bags, that will come in handy when you're adventuring and in your hotel room if they don't provide a mini-fridge. Above all, do not forget to bring plenty of birth control, unless you're hoping for a "honeymoon baby." How do you think so many couples "accidentally" get preggers on their honeymoon? There are no twenty-four hour drugstores in most romantic honeymoon spots, especially if you're visiting a remote island or mountaintop. Arrive prepared!

The Actual Job of Packing

While most of us would prefer not to mail any of our personal items to our wedding destinations, that may not be an option for a DIY bride and groom, especially if you're going on your honeymoon immediately following your wedding weekend. There's no way you can fit *everything you need* for your destination wedding and honeymoon into the amount of luggage an airline will let you bring without charging massive fees for extra baggage. That's where the box system comes in handy.

If you're an experienced packer and traveler, you'll be able to eyeball what's building up in that box of "Things to Pack" and realize when some of it needs to be relocated into the "Things to Ship" box. We'll talk more about how to handle shipping your personal items and your wedding décor and accoutrements (including your wedding gown) in Chapter 19.

You can't actually start packing your bags until a week or so before your wedding, and your clothing can't really be added to the suitcases (unless you're planning to steam or iron literally everything) until the day before your departure. But if you begin your packing list as soon as you begin your wedding planning, the actual job of loading it all in—without forgetting anything—will be significantly easier. I also guarantee you that you'll avoid *a lot* of fighting with your future spouse if the two of you aren't scrambling to find the elusive missing cufflink or racing through the mall sunglass shopping the week before you get married. That's the time when, as DIYers, you need to be confirming the details of your wedding with all the vendors and following up on all the other little things that a wedding planner would have done for you. Knowing ahead of time that you will not have time for the minutiae of wardrobe planning and packing in the month prior to your wedding should give you plenty of warning and time to get your shit together early in the game. Avoid the rush!

CHAPTER 16

⛤

CREATE A SUPPLIES-BY-EVENT LIST FOR EACH AND EVERY EVENT, AND SHOP AHEAD FOR THE THINGS YOU NEED TO SEND OR BRING

The Supplies-by-Event list is just as mission-critical to executing your wedding successfully as the Master Schedule. Without a carefully constructed, checked, and rechecked supply list that you use—first to make sure everything you need is headed to your destination, and second, to actually prep at the destination for what you need to take to events— there's no way you'll pull things off (at least not smoothly or easily). The goal is to arrive at your destination wholly prepared for all of the events you've planned and to have a shopping list of the things you couldn't ship that you have to go get for your events and welcome bags once you've arrived at the destination.

Our Supplies-by-Event list for each and every client lives right behind the schedules on our clipboards, and it's checked, double-checked, tweaked, and added to right up until the moment that we walk out the door for each and every wedding event. With our clients, we're often looking for them to bring certain items in their luggage, and we have to get our hands on that stuff when they arrive. Sometimes they forget to pack things and we have to add materials from our own warehouse to fill the holes. But we wouldn't know about it or realize we needed it if we didn't have that list.

"If It's Not on the List, It Doesn't Exist"

We have quite a team of folks who execute the setups and tear-downs at all of our professionally planned events. You're going to have that team too, but they're your friends and family. And you're not paying them based on performance.

Since you've planned the wedding yourself and most of them have never done anything quite like this, they're not going to real-ize what you're missing when you load up to go unless you have a copy of your list for everybody who might need it. My husband constantly preaches, "If it's not on the list, it doesn't exist!" And the interns quote him on this religiously because it's true. If we don't put it on the list and we don't have the item when we get to setup, the only person to blame is the one who approved the final list (usually me).

Making the List

DIY brides and grooms should approach creating the Supplies-by-Event list the same exact way they started their packing list—write each item down as you think about it. You might not think of it later on, and it might have been something small but impor-tant. Don't worry about putting it in order; just put it on the list with a dash and note about what it's going to be used for when you arrive. Once you have started to create your Master Schedule and you're confirming the activities you have actually planned, you'll create a fresh, new Supplies-by-Event list that is broken out by individual activity. Why is this so important? Because some of the things you're sending may need to be used more than once. It's not enough to "know" that you have double-sided tape and duct tape with you if you didn't put them in the box of supplies you brought to your beach party and that's where you need them. How are you going to tape down the tablecloths in a breeze or put fun signs on the rum punch jug if you left the tape back at your hotel or villa?

That's why so many basic items may appear in more than one place on your supply list for more than one event. You are going to have to move these things from one prep tub to the next before you load and go. And the only way on earth you will remember to do this, in all the chaos of DIYing your destination wedding after your guests have arrived, is if you faithfully stick to the list and check things off every time.

Supplies-by-Event lists will be extensive. They can be daunting, intimidating even. But they will also be your best friend when somebody helping set up your wedding asks, "Do you have fabric scissors?" while trying to tie bows on your napkins for your reception dinner. We all know you cannot cut ribbon (and have it look good) with regular scissors, right? If you don't have fabric scissors with you, you are screwed. And the chances that your reception venue (private villa or hotel), will even have fabric scissors, much less hunt them down to loan to you, is virtually nil. We often put things like fabric scissors on the list even if we've already rolled and tied bows on all the napkins, because you never know when something will happen and you have to create one more, or trim something. If you created or DIY'd something for your wedding, you need to bring backup parts and pieces along to setup in case you need it to make a repair.

If you're sending down family sailing cups to be used as centerpieces and handkerchiefs lovingly embroidered by the Mother of the Bride, they have to be packed carefully in order to arrive intact at your destination. And be sure to put them on the list of things to pack and bring back home! (Photos by Morris Malakoff)

Example List

To impress upon you the breadth and comprehensiveness of our Supplies-by-Event list, I'm going to show you a typical one from a real wedding planned by me and my staff. Don't let it freak you out, but *do use it* as a template and steal all the things off of it that you didn't think of yourself. I'm pretty positive that many of you will experience "aha!" moments when reading this. Of course, every wedding has different events so no two lists are exactly the same, but this is a great jumping-off point.

As you did with your wardrobe planning in Chapter 15, start by making a list of all the events that you're going to need to execute. And I mean put *absofreakinglutely everything* on that list, including your welcome bags and the goodies you're putting in them. You are going to be stressed and scattered when you arrive at your destination, unpacking, tracking down things you shipped to yourself, and dealing with guests as they begin to arrive (and trust me, some of them will come in days earlier than required if they're turning your destination wedding into their own vacation). Once they're there, they require your love and attention, even if they're earlier than you would have liked to greet them. So making sure you're organized on paper so you don't have to think too hard is an excellent idea.

Organize your list so that all the events are in order and you can follow it and check things off easily. The whole point of the exercise of creating a Supplies-by-Event list is to make your life as easy as possible. If it's not organized, you'll be chaotic trying to use it. For real, this is what a professional like me uses, and I think it's a key tool for DIYing your wedding successfully (comments in parentheses are my explanations or suggestions for you):

Welcome Bags—42 of each item, unless otherwise designated

- Welcome bags
- Welcome letters
- Maps and directions
- Local publications, advertisements, brochures, coupons (and any other info you can scrounge up)
- 2 bottles of water
- 2 packs of Advil
- 2 beach towels
- Chapstick (no, this bride didn't follow our suggestion to avoid things that melt, and yes, it was a gooey mess—but it's still my job to put it in the welcome bags)
- Sunscreen
- Bride and groom cookies ordered from pastry chef

Special welcome baskets for parents—2 total

- Basket or box with padding and ribbon to assemble on site
- Champagne (or a bottle of their favorite libation)
- Note from bride and groom
- Fresh fruit
- Chocolates (if you can find something not melted)
- Nuts

Wedding Rehearsal

- Ceremony plan (so you know what order things go in)
- Dr. Seuss vows (because if you practice with your real ones, you *will cry* at your wedding rehearsal—save the true ceremony for the wedding day)
- Rehearsal bouquet (that hilarious creation of ribbons from your bridal shower, pulled through the center of a paper plate)

Beach Party

- Beach permit
- Beach umbrellas
- Football
- Frisbees
- Volleyball net and poles
- Volleyball
- Air pump and needle
- Rafts
- Beach chairs
- 6 buffet tables
- 30 white plastic chairs
- 6 black trash bags
- 1 10x20 tent for guests—rental company will set up
- 1 10x10 tent for caterers—rental company will set up
- First-aid kit
- Bug repellent
- Plastic tablecloths for guest tables and catering tables, approx. 70 feet needed
- Packing tape
- Scissors
- Bathroom supplies
- Drill and auger for sinking beach umbrellas
- Flamingo inflatable beer cozies
- Basket or bucket to display cozies
- Pink and green straws—6 packs, bride is sending
- Pinwheels—bride is sending
- Pink cocktail napkins—bride is sending

Pig Roast—Rehearsal Dinner

- 2 buffet tables

- 36 tiki torches
- Fire extinguisher
- Extra tiki fuel (always get the kind with citronella oil in it because it wards off bugs)
- Sledgehammer (for sinking tiki bases so they're safely anchored)
- Fire pit
- Firewood
- Lighter fluid
- First-aid kit
- Trash bags
- Paper towels
- Windex
- Packing tape
- Double-sided tape
- Duct tape
- Scissors (fabric and regular)
- Signage (bathroom signs and "privacy" signs for bedroom doors if you're having the event in a venue where some guests are staying)
- 4 buffet tablecloths
- 6 large, white round tablecloths
- 3 small, white round tablecloths
- Long lighters (always bring more than one of things that could easily stop working)
- 10 cylinder vases for the dinner tables
- 20 votive candles (they never last as long as they should if you're dealing with breezes and ceiling fans)
- 75 sets of silverware rolled in napkins, tied with ribbon— bride is sending ribbon, pick up silverware from caterer
- 2 bathroom kits (decent antibacterial pump soap bottles and baskets with linen-like disposable hand towels—

nobody likes to use a wet hand towel that 60 other people have already used)

- Staff uniform shirts (if your catering servers and bartenders are cobbled together or don't usually wear uniforms, ask them to wear white shirts over black pants or skirts, with black shoes—be specific, or you may not be happy with the way they all appear and they will show up in your pictures)
- Laundry baskets for dirty tablecloths and napkins (you can use a trash bag—just don't get it mixed up with the actual garbage)
- Stain remover (better to spray tablecloths drenched in colorful cocktails and barbecue sauce *before* you toss them into the laundry bag—you may not be washing them immediately, and chances are they'll be permanently stained if you don't do a pre-emptive pre-spotting on everything)
- Palm tree cupcake toppers—bride is bringing with her
- 10 floral centerpieces for décor around the venue

Ceremony
- Programs—bride is sending
- Ceremony plans (an extra copy of the actual ceremony in case the minister forgets it and a page listing in what order everyone should be sent down the aisle)
- Bridal emergency bag (explained in great detail in Chapter 21)
- Paper towels and Windex (more often than not, we have to clean every chair we get from the rental company—they're not what you want to ask your guests to sit in without a good wipe-down first)
- Bouquets to be delivered to bridal suite
- Boutonnieres for the gentlemen

- Petals for aisle
- Flower girl floral crown with streaming ribbons
- Flower girl basket with petals
- Ring bearer pillow with fake rings attached
- 12 bouquets for aisle chairs
- 70 chairs—rental company is bringing
- Extra ivory ribbon for chair bouquets
- Wire ties to mount bouquets or ribbon
- Wire cutters
- 75 monogrammed handkerchiefs
- Basket for distributing monogrammed handkerchiefs—put extras on guestbook table after ceremony
- 70 fans with personalized tags to put on guests' chairs
- 5 tiki torches to put in arc behind ceremony site
- Extra tiki fuel
- Sledgehammer (for sinking tiki torches and tent pegs)
- Fire extinguisher (no, really, you should purchase a small one when you get to your destination and have it on hand at all of your events—you can't ship them, and you might not find the one at your venue that actually works in an emergency)
- Pink tulle to tie around tiki torches
- Extra pink tulle to rope off aisle
- Fabric scissors

Reception
- 24 tiki torches to light pathways and put around the pool
- Extra tiki fuel
- Sledgehammer
- Fire extinguisher
- 2 ladders

- 4 black trash bags
- White lights for decorating
- Extension cords
- Power strips
- Wire ties to anchor lights
- Wire cutters
- Paper towels
- Windex
- Packing tape
- Double-sided tape
- Duct tape
- First-aid kit
- Radios/headsets (if you have some radios at home, bring them because they might come in handy—our entire team wears them at all events so we're not shouting instructions at each other, but DIYers don't really have to worry about that so much)
- Long lighters
- Luggage tag favors—bride is sending

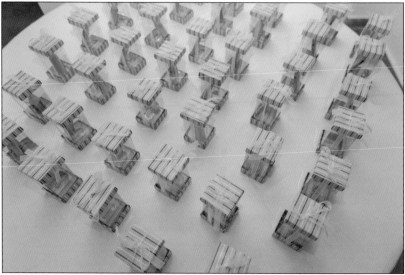

Wedding favors should be pre-packed or boxed/wrapped ahead of shipping them to your destination so they can be easily displayed on a table at the reception. Plan in advance whether you're going to be bringing back the extras—or at least taking the gifts out of the boxes to save space shipping. (Top and bottom photos by EP Anderson Photography, middle photo by Morris Malakoff)

- Place cards—bride is sending
- Place card holders—bride is sending
- Escort cards—bride is sending (escort cards tell the guest what table they're assigned to, and the place cards are at the seats on the table they've been assigned; however, you can simply do place cards and let the guests choose their own seats at the table—it's much easier and less formal)
- Escort card holders—bride is sending
- Table numbers—bride is sending
- Table number holders
- Place card chart (always have multiple copies of this available because your caterer will likely not have brought his own even if you sent it ahead to him—you'll need to provide it on your wedding day)
- Cake knife
- Fabric scissors
- Regular scissors
- Flower scissors
- Flowers for top of the cake
- 7 special votive holders—bride is sending
- 7 light pink tea lights—1 on each table, sweetheart table, and cake table
- LED lights for inside Chinese lanterns
- Fishing line for hanging lanterns (make sure you bring strong-enough stuff)
- 10 green Chinese lanterns
- 10 silver Chinese lanterns
- 10 white Chinese lanterns
- 18 pink Chinese lanterns
- Picture matting for guest book with special pens—bride is sending

Topping your cake with fresh flowers or decorating your dessert table to match your bouquet or décor is an easy way to give it a finished look. You can also use your bouquets, decorative fans, and family pictures to decorate the cake table. (Top photo by Saul Padua, bottom photo by EP Anderson Photography)

Monogrammed table runners made by a family member or friend can be a very personalized touch. (Photo by Morris Malakoff)

- 5 packs of decorative straws for bar—bride is sending
- 75 monogrammed napkins pre-folded as bride designated—bride is sending
- 2 monogrammed table runners—1 for sweetheart table, 1 for cake table—bride is sending
- 8 round white linen tablecloths
- Monogrammed cocktail napkins for bar—bride is sending
- 75 take-away cake bags
- 75 take-away cake forks
- Monogrammed stickers to seal cake bags—bride is sending
- Floral centerpieces for dinner tables and cake table
- Underwater LED lights for the bottom of the swimming pool
- 16 medium white candles
- 24 small white candles
- 12 small glass votive holders

Underwater lighting can make for spectacular pictures and amazing décor at a wedding with a pool at the venue. Disposable underwater LED lights are invisible until it becomes dark outside, and then it looks like a million stars in the bottom of the swimming pool. (Photo by Morris Malakoff)

- 14 medium glass candle holders
- 13 clear glass votive holders
- 2 spherical glass candle holders—bride is sending
- Props for the photo booth
- Sign with instructions for DIY photo booth
- Sparklers
- Sparkler bucket (put water in it and have it on hand for hot sparklers after usage)
- Blow torch (you can't travel with these, but you can buy and bring the torch part that you put on top of a camping-size can of propane you buy at your destination—we find these significantly more efficient for lighting seventy-five to one hundred and fifty sparklers in under five minutes so

Brooke and Jason thoroughly enjoyed their sparkler tunnel, a perfect escape from the wedding reception and not that difficult to plan if you remember the safety supplies! (Photo by Saul Padua Photography)

the first half of the tunnel doesn't go dark before the bride and groom finish dancing their way through—you can use long lighters, but it takes *forever* to get all the sparklers lit)

If you're a normal DIY bride and groom, that list just freaked you out completely. Or you're thinking that you're not going to need all that stuff because you're hiring caterers and rental people to do it all for you. *You still need to make the list.* Where I was writing "bride is sending," you should be writing "caterer will provide" or "rental company will bring and set up." And keep those things on your lists.

Make separate lists by vendor to review with each of them ahead of time to make sure your expectations are on par with what they're planning to bring. You need to know if the caterers are

Heather and James had fun drawing hearts with their sparklers at the end of the tunnel, making a fantastic picture to have forever. (Photo by Morris Malakoff)

providing the linens or not. Will it be paper or fabric, and which did you want? This exercise in getting your events organized in a Supplies-by-Event format will also help you make sure your vendors are equally organized. In more remote destinations, you may have hired some people who have less experience at this than you would like, but if you let them know what you need, they'll do their best to provide it. Or they'll tell you no and you'll have to decide if you want to take care of it yourself.

When the Supplies-by-Event list is as complete as possible (and it's never actually finished because you'll add things you think of at the last minute—you must write it down as you think of it or you will forget it), you need to make a packing list for yourself of these items that have to be shipped. You'll also need a separate list of things that you need to buy when you get to your destination.

That should be a top priority when you get there. Arrive, dump your stuff, and start that shopping. Sometimes, in a remote location without any big-box stores, you're going to have to go to ten different places to find everything on your list. And you might be out hunting for some other things after that.

How to Find What You Need at Your Destination

Your best resource for saving time shopping at your destination is the caretaker, property manager, or hotel manager you're working with—tell them what you need and ask where to find it. Even if they didn't seem helpful ahead of your arrival, if you're friendly and sweet and excited in person when you're finally there, they will help you. It doesn't hurt to give them a tip ($20 is fine) after they've been helpful. They'll probably even offer to help you with additional questions if you call them. Remember, time is money and a big, enthusiastic thank-you goes a long way too. Without the actual people at your destination on your side, you're screwed if something breaks or doesn't show up and you need help. Build those relationships early.

Making Prep Tubs

We make a "prep tub" for each and every event we execute at Weddings in Vieques. You're not going to have twenty spare plastic tubs at your destination, so plan on using the bigger boxes that you shipped things down for this project (if, of course, they arrived sturdy enough to re-use). Bring sharpies and a roll of wide masking tape (go ahead, take a second and add those to your packing list) and label each box as you designate its purpose. Every event gets its own prep tub, even if you're only putting one or two things in it. You can always downsize when you're finished prepping if you didn't need that much space. At our office, we have plastic tubs of just about every size for this purpose.

This is what the shelves look like for just one wedding planned by our office when the bride sends lots of DIY décor ahead of her event, in addition to the supplies we really need. Plan on needing this much space to prep your own wedding supplies at your destination.

Label the box "Rehearsal Dinner" or "Wedding Ceremony" as you start to fill it. For some events, you're going to need a whole lot of boxes. You can even list the contents on the side of the box if you're finding it confusing. The most important list you'll make when you're actually filling up your prep tubs on location at your destination is the list of things that have to be moved from one event tub to another. For example, we have more than one set of fabric scissors and more than one roll of duct tape and scads of long lighters at our office. When we prep, the only thing we seem to have to move from tub to tub is the first-aid kit, because we keep those pretty freshly restocked and only have a few of them. But you are your own wedding planner, and you will probably bring only one of everything that you need, and *a lot of it* will need to be transferred to the next event's prep tub after the first event is completed.

You will be tired after each and every wedding event you DIY, and you will be tempted just to toss everything back into a box to deal with later instead of tackling it that night when you get back to your accommodations. *Don't do that.* You have to pay attention to where the scissors go after you use them, and the staple gun, and the duct tape. Otherwise, your cleanup crew will accidentally leave them behind and you will be screwed the next morning when you're trying to set up another event.

Shopping for Your Wedding Supplies

This can be tricky for DIY brides and grooms because you don't really have a safe and reliable landing point for everything you are shipping. Frequently, you can ship ahead to a hotel or to a property caretaker, but you can only send things a couple of weeks ahead. You can't really ship directly from someplace you're shopping online because most of the time those boxes don't arrive labeled so that the hotel will have any idea who they're for when they open them.

Our interns are posing with the average stack of boxes that may arrive on any day in Vieques, just to give you an idea of how much room all the DIY stuff you're shipping takes up and how much it will cost you to send it.

We let our clients start shipping to us a couple of months ahead of their weddings, and with busy wedding months like April and May, our office gets really, really full. And we have a big space! You will accrue a ton of stuff to ship for your wedding—have a plan for what you're going to do with it. If you don't have the space, see if you can borrow some garage or basement space from one of your parents and have things sent directly to them. You can get it all organized to ship from there.

When to Shop for Your Wedding Supplies

You should have completed your shopping for everything you have on your Supplies-by-Event list at least sixty days ahead of your wedding, and probably earlier. There's no reason you can't start gathering all the parts and pieces early—duct tape and Sharpies don't go bad in new packaging. Open tape rolls becomes a gluey mess in tropical humidity, and if you've never seen a previously-opened Sharpie explode, trust me that you don't want it to happen in a box of wedding supplies. You should be picking things up on sale as much as possible as you proceed with your DIY wedding planning.

Just make sure you put them in the "Things to Ship" box as soon as they enter the house, and don't steal them to use before your wedding. That's the best way to accidentally leave things behind. Don't tell yourself, "Oh, we have duct tape. I'll grab that." You don't need the stress of trying to find tape and Sharpies and scissors to steal from your house to ship to your destination. Also, when you do that, you don't have them in your house for a few weeks before your wedding. Buy new! It's okay to keep the new ones at home and ship the old ones you already had. Just make sure you're not shipping dried-up glue or gummed-up tape. And put everything in *individual* zip-lock bags in case of the aforementioned Sharpie explosion.

CHAPTER 17

଼ଓ

CREATE A VENDOR CHECKLIST
AND KEEP IT UPDATED

*Y*ou should have created, through the process of planning so far, a general vendor checklist that you're going to use to keep yourself sane and organized through the wedding planning. In Chapter 3, I talked about how to track your vendor payment and contract information. That's a great jumping off point, but there's a lot more that you have to keep track of as DIY brides and grooms.

If complicated Excel spreadsheets make you happy, by all means, make one for yourself. If you'd rather keep things a little more simple, you can create a binder with pages for each vendor. Keep your original contracts in a file someplace safe, but feel free to include copies of them in the binder should you need to refer to them at any point during your wedding events. If a caterer tells you that your barbecue was supposed to last two hours as he's shutting down the bar early, and you know damned well that it was a contract for three hours, you'll have a copy right there to show him. If you have to scramble to find the information, you're going to get stressed out and upset and not enjoy the event at all.

If a vendor does mess up something and you have to point out the flaw in the contract so they can fix it on the fly, be nice about it, no matter how angry you are. You always catch more flies with honey, and event planning is no exception. Don't yell at the vendor in front of anybody. Take them aside, show them the error, and be nice about it. They're going to be more willing to fix it (and probably embarrassed about the error) if you're nice about it. If they are publicly embarrassed or feel disrespected, that contract might mean nothing to them and they'll ignore it. What are the odds you're actually going to come back and sue them for it? It probably won't be worth it. The threat of consequences to vendors from DIY brides and grooms is almost nil—the only thing you can really do is trash them online afterwards. And a lot of the vendors you'll be using aren't even listed on wedding websites that take reviews. So just be nice and try to get them to fix it.

Once you've set up different pages (or columns) for each of your vendors, keep track of every conversation and email exchanged. Set up folders in your email inbox by vendor name so that you can quickly refer to them if necessary. You don't have to print out *everything* if you just make sure you can access it at a moment's notice. Note when you pay them, but also note when you discussed their list of things to bring, and yours.

Write down questions you need to ask them next time you communicate about your wedding plans. Vendors would prefer to get one comprehensive email, or do one organized conference call, to review as much as possible all at the same time. A barrage of emails and voicemails in the vendor's inbox from needy brides and grooms just makes the vendor start to dread those upcoming weddings. They have multiple clients, and keeping organized when a bride sends you every random thought about her cake will make the pastry chef insane. Sending her seventeen pictures of cakes that don't look anything alike will frustrate her. She can't give you a bid on a cake until you actually know what flavor each tier should be, and if you want filling, and whether it's frosted with buttercream or fondant. Use these pages to organize your questions in a manner that will streamline vendor communications and not be just plain annoying.

Florists suffer much like pastry chefs, especially when they're dealing directly with brides and grooms with no intermediary like a wedding planner to help them narrow down the list of things they "like," "want," and "need" into a reasonable slate of things they can actually afford. I own a flower shop on Vieques Island too, so I do a lot of wedding flowers for brides who are not my planning clients. The most painful thing to receive is an email with fifty different bouquets attached, none of which resemble each other in any way. You might have everything from pink to blue, from round and front-held to massively cascading, all attached to one email that's titled "Bouquets I Like." Well that's just great, but could you be a little more specific, please?

Only the bride and groom can narrow down the zillion pics on their ideas boards on Pinterest to send a vendor a realistic expression of what they envision for their wedding. Some brides start out thinking garden party and end up going elegant and modern after they fall in love with a specific wedding gown they don't think fits the décor they've planned. As a DIY bride and groom with no wedding planner to keep the individual vendors from killing you (or worse, refusing to work with you), it's important that you take specific notes about what you want and clip exact pictures of things that represent what you like. It's okay to send three bouquet pictures and indicate you like the color of one, the shape of another, and the way the stems are wrapped in the third. But sharing a link to every random thought you've had since you started planning your wedding is absurd and unrealistic. If you don't know what you like, how is a vendor supposed to help you? We're wedding vendors—not magicians and not psychics. Take notes, narrow down the list of things you really like, and then get the bid from your vendor. With some vendors you can let them know you wish to use them and then have some time to gather information for them to prepare a bid; don't move ahead until you're ready to do so. When you do, take notes on everything.

Have these notes in front of you when you talk to your vendors. I cannot tell you how irritating it is when a bride actually sends me pictures of what she says is the "exact" décor she wants and then she can't remember what she sent me when we talk. Sometimes I have to email them back their own pictures! Be organized, and you are more likely to get what you want out of your vendors. If you're confused about what you want, imagine how they feel trying to interpret your wishes from thousands of miles away!

CHAPTER 18

&CB

PAY ALL YOUR OUTSTANDING BALANCES ON TIME, OR AS SOON AS YOU GET AN INVOICE

*W*hile we're talking about how to deal with your vendors, let's talk about how to handle the money for everything you're doing for your wedding. This is important because, if you screw it up, a vendor has every right to say you missed a deadline, breached the contract, and they are no longer servicing your wedding. And there won't be one single thing you can do about it. "It's not fair," you'll whine. But really, is it fair to hire somebody to provide a service and then fail to pay them by the agreed-upon date? No, it's not.

Starting Off on the Right Foot with Vendors
Some wedding services are pretty clear-cut, like the DJ or band, for example. The service costs X amount per hour, and your contract will be for a specific amount of time. They will send you a contract and you should *always return the contract with the deposit within seven days* unless there is a different specified deadline. If you need

an extra week for some reason, reach out to the vendor and explain your predicament and ask if it's all right to send payment at a later, mutually agreed-upon date. If it's going to be within a week, you're probably all good. If you're asking for an extension of more than that, don't expect to get it. You'll probably be told that they'll be happy to take your wedding contract *if they haven't already booked another wedding for that date* by the time you have the money to pay your deposit. It's all business, and you wouldn't believe how many brides try to hold dates with multiple vendors at the same time. We know the game, and we don't play it. At least, experienced vendors won't. If somebody is too willing to give you leeway, it may be because they don't have other clients and aren't really experienced with doing weddings.

Reality Check: If you don't have the money for vendor deposits when you sign a contract, you have no business booking those vendors yet. And if you're DIYing your wedding and can't pay the deposits, you're probably getting out of your financial comfort zone and should stop everything until you get your monetary ducks in a row. It's fine to do your research, contact vendors for pricing, and check their availability, but do not ask them to save the date for you or send you a contract unless you're prepared to pay the deposit.

That's why I tell every client that I will not hold their wedding date (and in the case of flowers-only clients, guarantee their pricing), until I have received the signed contract and deposit. That's when we mark the wedding calendar in my office—you don't exist without a deposit.

Keep Up Your End of the Deal with Your Vendors

With almost every wedding vendor, you're going to have deadlines for your planning. For the DJ or other musicians, it's the playlist (and "do not play" list) that is due to them by a certain date. With caterers, it's the final headcount by a certain date so they can plan their staffing and ordering (destination wedding vendors have special challenges related to bringing in supplies for your wedding). If you miss a deadline, it sets off a chain of unintended consequences for you. Remember that raw bar you were so desperate for? You might have to forego that if you missed the caterer's deadline and he couldn't order in the oysters.

Make sure you put down the details of what information is due (not just what money is due) in your spreadsheet or information page for tracking your vendors. Set reminders on your calendar. Do whatever you have to do to keep yourself on track. You chose to DIY your wedding, right? And you acknowledge that there are plenty of professional wedding planners out there who do this for a living, right? So if you decide to DIY your own wedding planning, the best way to approach the task it to treat it like a job, albeit a fun one.

Set goals and deadlines like you would for an assignment at work—and stick to them! If you're getting overwhelmed and your fiancé has his or her head in the sand, yank them back out of that hole and tell them you need help. You took on this DIY project together and you cannot do it alone (unless you promised your fiancé you wouldn't ask him to do anything, in which case, call your best friend or Mom). You are trying to accomplish the same thing that real wedding planners spend hours, day after day, doing for their clients. DIYers must expect to put in the same amount of time planning their wedding (if not more) than any seasoned professional. Experienced planners don't have to do all the research you do—they already have vetted vendor lists they trust.

Block Out the Time to Actually
Do Your Planning Homework

DIY brides and grooms actually have a lot more work to do than a professional planning team, because the couple doesn't live in the destination or know whom to trust. Make the time to plan your wedding, or call "uncle" and hire somebody to step in and finish it for you if you find yourself up against the wall a few months out. If you start DIY planning early enough and complete the tasks as quickly as they hit your to-do list, you should be able to DIY your wedding just fine. Lifelong procrastinators with the DIY bug should hire a wedding planner and stick to hand-crafting their invitations and favors. Wedding planning is a real job (when it's done properly), and when you decide to DIY your wedding, it's like adding a second job to your life until the wedding date finally arrives. Accept that and move on. You're going to be spending a lot of your free time playing wedding planner right up to and through your wedding weekend.

Final Payment Due Dates

Every contract tells you, very specifically, when the final payment is due. For most destination vendors, the final balance is due, with the final headcount, before or at the thirty-day-out mark. That's because they have to spend the money to bring in the supplies for your event and they want to make sure your wedding is still happening.

Some vendors should be paid exactly on time no matter what. Nothing is changing about your music contracts, wedding cake, cookie wedding favors, minister, transportation, or event permits, as well as many other services. That means you should have those checks in the mail (or be emailing them credit card authorizations) one week prior to the deadline. There is no excuse for anything to be late. It's just sloppy to risk losing a wedding vendor so close to your wedding date because you were too busy and important to send the check.

What Vendors Think

It's nerve-wracking when you invoice a client for the final balance and they don't pay on time. Not every vendor sends a final invoice, because the contract tells you what you're supposed to do and it's your job to actually make the payment. They weren't required to remind you unless you had that written into your contract.

When you do not pay your wedding vendors on time, we panic a little bit. We've held that wedding date for months, put in hours (in some cases) helping you revise and revise and revise until you were happy with your plan, and suddenly we're not getting paid! What's that about? My immediate thought is that the client doesn't have the money, and that's what all my colleagues in the wedding business think, too. Why would any wedding couple miss their payment deadlines and risk not having a photographer if they had the money to pay the bills? That's just crazy.

Sometimes the money is the problem, but more often than not, brides and grooms get lazy and simply take their time to pay their tabs. They do not realize that a wedding vendor *really might cancel* based on breach of contract if they're a few days late with a payment—especially if they get a call for another gig the same night as yours. Why would they keep holding your wedding date open with an unpaid balance when they have another client ready to pay 100 percent up front right then and there? And because you missed your deadline, they get to keep your deposit too. It's win-win for the vendor. Sounds mean, right? That's only because you're the bride and groom, and you can't help feeling a little bit like the world revolves around you in the last months before your wedding. To a wedding vendor, you're just another client who didn't pay their bill. It's purely business, and if you miss the deadline, you've handled it badly.

Getting Your Money Together

Even if a vendor does need to invoice you before you can pay—a caterer who has to revise your numbers based on head count, for example—you need to be getting the money together before that invoice arrives. Part of your responsibility as a DIY wedding couple is to manage your wedding budget. You signed every contract. Theoretically, you're keeping the spreadsheet I recommended up to date. You don't need the "final final" number back from the vendor to know how much money you're going to owe if you can do basic math. You can eyeball it pretty well based on the paperwork you have at your disposal.

When you get to that sixty-day-out mark, it's time to deal with the financial matters. Calculate what you're going to owe (estimating where necessary), and get the money together so you have it ready to go. For some couples who plan to put everything on credit cards (if vendors at your destination take plastic), pay off the cards ahead of time. Make sure you have enough room on your cards to make all the necessary payments. If you don't, either call your bank and see if you can get a limited-time credit extension or start paying some of your vendors earlier so you can pay off balances before the next charge comes through. It's not uncommon for one of my clients who owes tens of thousands of dollars to me and wedding vendors to provide final payment information with very specific instructions about how much can be charged when—X amount of money per day if they're using debit cards, for example, or, Y being the limit on the card, they need twenty-four hours in between charges to pay the card back to zero again.

In this day and age, after a recession that caused so many credit card providers to lower credit limits, this is not an uncommon problem. Your vendor should be happy as a clam to work with you to break up the charges, *if you contact him in advance*. If you wait until a few days after the payment deadline and then ask them to break up the charges over a period of a week, however, you may not find them so receptive.

If you have to move money out of investment accounts, cash in stock options (I did that), or get a check from your parents to cover their commitment for your wedding festivities, do that ahead of time (at least a month before the money will actually be due). It's only fair to give plenty of notice to your parents, who may also be moving the money from another set-aside account to help with your wedding and who may need a few days to make transfers and write the check.

Paying a Late Invoice

So let's say you had your financial act together and were ready to pay all your vendors by the deadline, but the caterer or florist or whoever failed to send you the revised final invoice for the balance you have due—how should you handle that?

First thing you should do is email the vendor to make sure they haven't forgotten about your wedding and are working on getting you the final numbers. Anybody who sounds too lackadaisical about the final payment should make you a little bit nervous. They should need and want your final payment, and that's the only way you can guarantee they're going to be servicing your wedding. But if they say they're working on it, give them a couple more days. You never know how the timing of when you gave them your final numbers may have coincided with a week when they were catering four other weddings. All wedding vendors operate on the theory that the brides and grooms getting married that week get absolute first priority and the most attention. So you might have to wait a few extra days, even though it's making you nervous.

It's perfectly okay for a DIY bride or groom to contact the vendor to ask when they can expect their final balance. Just be nice about it and not overly pushy unless it's the second or third time you've had to follow up (in which case, a phone call is in order if you don't get an almost immediate response and explanation).

But here's the trick about bugging the vendor for the invoice—when you get it, he or she will expect nearly immediate payment! Yes, you bugged them for weeks, so you might think they're going to cut you some slack to get the payment out. Wrong-o. Unless your contract says otherwise, the balance due on your invoice is due pretty much upon demand if you're past the date the money was due—even if the delay was the vendor's fault. Sometimes DIY brides and grooms blame the vendor when the cause of the problem was actually their own initial delay in giving final numbers or information to that vendor. If they'd turned it in the week they were supposed to, the vendor would have had plenty of time to revise and send the clients an invoice. Your delay of a week to ten days (just a little delay in your head) in submitting the information may mean that you're suddenly asking a vendor to stop what he's doing and concentrate on re-running the numbers for your wedding while he's in the middle of trying to execute a job for another bride and groom. You are not their only client. Their world has not stopped to revolve around you. So if you don't submit information when you're supposed to, you're assuming that vendor will drop everything for you when you get around to it. That's not what happens. Sometimes it is the vendor's fault that the invoice is late and you have a right to be irritated, but don't let that irritation cloud your judgment and risk an important element of your wedding.

Just pay the vendor as fast as possible and treat them respectfully and they will probably appreciate you as a client even more.

True Life: Every vendor expects full payment as soon as he gives you the invoice, especially if you've been dogging him for it. Within twenty-four hours would be considered reasonable in the industry, as it gives you plenty of time to double-check his final numbers and question any discrepancies. The fact that you just got the invoice (late, even) doesn't give you a timeout or a rain delay. It simply means you've been denied the ability to coast for a week before you make a payment. Regardless of when you got the invoice or who was at fault for the delay, you're in breach of contract because you haven't paid the balance as soon as it's handed to you. Could you fight it in court? Probably. Would you win? Depends where you are. But do you really want to have that happen between you and a wedding vendor right before your wedding? It's the worst possible vibe to have working at your wedding. Know when your bills are due and be prepared to pay them within a day, regardless of when they're actually sent to you.

Cash and Tips

This is also the time to figure out how much tip money you need to bring with you to your destination for your vendors. Use checks for the businesses you've contracted so you can carry less cash. Know how much cash you're going to need and whether your bank card will actually let you withdraw funds at your destination. Advise your bank and credit card companies of where you're getting married, so you won't have fraud alerts popping up every time you go to use your cards or get cash. Put the cash for tips (and any cash required for final vendor payments) into labeled envelopes and store them somewhere safe. You will be so happy you're not counting out money all over a bed and stuffing envelopes the night before your wedding weekend begins when you simply take the envelopes out of the room safe and have them ready to go.

Now that we've completely tackled how to DIY your wedding finances and satisfy your vendors, let's move on to some general wedding "housekeeping" and some fun wedding topics!

CHAPTER 19

ಐ ೞ

SHIPPING THINGS AHEAD SO THEY'RE WAITING WHEN YOU ARRIVE AT YOUR DESTINATION

*T*he day I shipped the last box from DC to Vieques for my own DIY destination wedding was a glorious one. I got an entire room's worth of space back in my house when all those boxes left. I also spent twice as much on shipping as on my wedding cake, but that's the reality of DIYing a wedding. Without a wedding planner onsite at your destination to tell you what you do and do not have to send, you're working blind and it's better to ship anything you're not sure about.

Determining Your Drop Point for Shipments
How you ship, what you ship, when you ship, and how much you ship depends entirely on where you are getting married and who is accepting your packages.

Shipping to Hotels
If you've booked at a hotel, they'll probably be happy to receive your boxes within a limited number of days prior to the wedding.

Believe it or not, they don't really have a lot of storage space for your wedding things, and you don't want to risk your boxes getting lost or misplaced. *Do not mail anything to a hotel without designating it to the attention of a specific person who has agreed to receive your boxes.* Mailing it to yourself weeks ahead of your wedding won't work either—don't expect them to hold everything without making prior arrangements with an actual person at the destination. Hotels are busy places—the bigger, the busier—and they get mail for random guests who are no longer there all the time. And they tell UPS, FedEx, or the mailman to simply return it to sender, or it gets tossed in a room of other unclaimed luggage and things left behind. Good luck finding it when you arrive.

Shipping to a Property Manager or Caretaker

If you've lucked out and the property manager, rental agent, or caretaker of the private villa you rented has agreed to accept packages for you, make sure you manage expectations and get their address exactly right.

If you're shipping thirty-two big boxes like I did (I told you I was the original DIY destination bride), they need to know that and agree to it. They may want to charge you a fee for all the time they'll be spending running to and from the post office. After all, it's not really their job. They don't *have to* let you mail anything to them. The process is time-consuming at many destinations. Mail doesn't all arrive together just because you mailed it the same day. Agree to pay a reasonable fee (yes, a couple hundred bucks is reasonable for twenty boxes when you consider they're going to get them trickling in, let you know when they arrive, store them, and deliver them all to your villa before you get there). If they agree to do it and don't charge you a fee, be prepared with a sizeable cash tip when you arrive and find your shipments secure and waiting.

What I Tell All My Clients

I've already confessed to the massive client guide I send to all my brides and grooms, but I didn't tell you that I'm constantly answering questions with the words "that's in the client guide." I'm polite about it, but seriously, I'm not going to spend another thirty minutes emailing you the damned instructions again when you have them. I just resend the client guide and refer them to the correct page number.

Occasionally, clients do not actually read the shipping instructions in the guide (because I only wrote them to entertain myself, not to help them, right?), and they haul all the stuff to the post office and then slam me with text messages demanding my address, info about how it should be shipped, and a million other questions—in real time. If I'm on a conference call with another client right then, or actually running a wedding rehearsal, I might not respond fast enough that they're not inconvenienced. By the same token, you should get clear shipping instructions from whomever you're mailing your packages to *before* you head out to mail things, or you may find yourself in the same position. *Never guess* an address to save yourself a second trip. You might not see your boxes again.

In addition to providing my correct address information in the client guide, I also get very, very specific about how to go about packing and shipping. What's amazing is how much still arrives badly packaged and broken. I had one bride who shipped her grandmother's wedding champagne flutes in a shoe box inside another box with absolutely zero padding around the glasses in the shoe box. As you can imagine, they broke. It actually looked like a box of rock salt when we opened it up, it had been shaken up so badly. Crystal has to be packaged properly and, even if you insure it, the post office will not reimburse you if the pictures show you didn't package things properly in the first place. Never mind the fact that family heirlooms like those champagne flutes are literally irreplaceable.

I'm going to share the actual text of my client guide with you here just to demonstrate how specific and direct I am with my clients. Although this information will change based on where you're getting married, the gist of it will give you the information you need to get for shipping things to wherever you are getting married, and tell you how to go about successfully sending everything.

Use the Pony Express

You should mail everything to me via priority (US) mail. Those flat-rate envelopes and boxes work great. It's the best way to ensure that checks and contracts and everything else for your wedding arrive in a timely manner on the island. Pick up some extra flat-rate packaging the next time you're at the post office mailing me something and keep them handy. I DO notice when you use snail mail and it drives me insane, because it usually means checks arrive well after deadline.

If you have to send something UPS or FedEx, be sure to put my cell phone number on the mailing form. Be aware that each of those services only delivers to Vieques a few times a week, so the US Mail is always your fastest and most cost-effective method of mailing anything to me. If you do use another service, please give me a heads-up so I know when to expect the package. I have the cell numbers of the guys who deliver for them (there's only one of each) and I'll stay on top of it. Put my cell phone number all over the box too—whatever works!

Tracking Your Packages

Just because the postal tracking (or UPS or FedEx) says a package has arrived here, that *does not* mean it has. It just means it has made it as far as San Juan. That's the facts, and there's nothing you can do about it. If we tell you it's not here but the online postal tracking system says it has been delivered, we're not making it up. We have no motive to lie. In order to manage your shipping expectations:

- US Next-Day Mail—2 to 3 days
- US Priority Mail—5 to 7 days
- Regular mail—3 to 4 weeks for packages, 3 days to 3 weeks for first-class letters
- UPS/FedEx—each delivers only a few times a week to the island . . . usually. Sometimes it's more frequently, but we can never count on that. Next-day services with both of those shipping services mean that if you mail it no later than Tuesday, we should get it by Friday . . . maybe. Once in a very rare while, a package arrives overnight—something considered cause for celebration in the islands.

What to Do About Things You Need to Ship to the Island

You can start sending me things for your wedding *45 days out* from the wedding date—no sooner, unless we've made special arrangements ahead of time. I don't have enough storage space to handle it for longer than that. As it is, I have to spread it out all over my office when I unpack it all and prep for your wedding. If you're sending me nine boxes, imagine how many boxes other brides are sending. During a busy wedding month, it's like a wedding warehouse around here.

Please keep in mind the Caribbean's tropical environment when you ship. Unless you've made special prior arrangements with me, you aren't going to have temperature-controlled storage here, so some things you might want to send for welcome bags can become a gooey, disgusting mess. Other things can mildew or mold in the humidity. Make sure you talk to me about exactly what you're sending so I can help do damage control before something bad happens.

How to Pack Things You're Shipping

Package the contents of all of your boxes like you're sending them to the other side of the world. You wouldn't believe the condition some things are in when we receive them. Once we received a postal service bag with everything in it from a box that exploded. Who knows what was lost! Use lots of tape—and tape the seams too. Make sure you pad everything properly. Bubble wrap is your friend—use it! If you don't package glass properly, it will arrive broken. Sometimes it's too late for you to ship replacement items in time for your wedding, and some family heirlooms cannot be replaced. Insure, insure, insure everything for at least the minimum available. From experience, we think they treat well-insured packages a little bit better.

Be smart about what you mail to the Caribbean. Chocolate melts. Candles melt. Chapsticks melt. So do lots of other things that don't begin with the letter "C."

Please put a list of the contents of the box inside the lid before you tape it shut to save me time when I'm opening it. If I'm not going to know what you're sending because it's something you haven't mentioned to me, then tell me what it's for on the box inventory. Otherwise, I have to email you and ask, every time. It is all right to email your Inventory List to me too—but you need to make sure there is a page included in each box mailed. If you're sending several boxes, number them and let us know how many are coming (as in actually writing the numbers "1 of 3," "2 of 3," etc. on the boxes as you ship them).

Do not ship me anything that isn't supposed to be shipped. Do not mail me illegal drugs. Do not mail me fireworks. Do not mail me anything else on the "no-no" list at the post office. This has happened in the past and, let us be clear, we will not deliver your illegal substances to your accommodations with your welcome basket. We will turn them over to the authorities.

Please don't ship boxes that weigh more than forty pounds or are too unwieldy or large for one person to carry, unless you have made special arrangements. There will be a labor fee assessed if I have to send an entire crew to town to pick up your boxes.

Transporting Your Wedding Gown to Your Destination

It is not impossible to travel with your wedding gown, but it is a handful, literally. More of my brides carry their dresses than ship ahead, but plenty of them mail them too. I kind of get a kick out of having wedding gowns hanging around the office during a busy wedding month. Whichever way you decide you want to get your wedding gown to your destination, there's a specific way to do it.

A wedding gown doesn't arrive at the destination looking as fantastic as Vanessa's did unless you take very special care getting it there, whether you're shipping it ahead or carrying it on the plane with you. (Photo by Saul Padua Photography)

Carrying-On Your Wedding Gown

Some brides won't even consider letting that dress out of their sight for the time it would take to ship it, and they don't trust that it will actually arrive (or don't have someone reliable on the other end to receive it). Most DIY brides *should not* ship their dresses. You can easily hand-carry your dress on your trip, but I have some great tips that make it even easier.

- Arrive early at the airport for check-in and be super-sweet and excited about the fact that you're going to get married. Sometimes you luck into an upgrade, and believe me, traveling with a wedding gown in First Class is easy as pie.
- If you're traveling in coach and have the option to pay a little extra for early boarding, spend the money!

- When you're going through security, please ask TSA to hand-check your gown and ask them to put on fresh gloves before doing so. Female agents will understand; men may give you dirty looks. But God only knows what's on those gloves they're about to run all over your dress—better to annoy them a little than to have your wedding gown arrive at your destination covered in strange stains.
- Get to your gate early and check in with the gate agents. When you see them organizing your flight, go up and introduce yourself and ask, all sweet and excited, if it's possible to board earlier because you're so worried about your wedding gown. You might have some extras of the cutesy DIY treats you're transporting handy—everybody likes a cookie, right? Make friends if you can, and be polite if you can't. Whatever you do, don't go Bridezilla on them if they tell you that they can't help you get that dress someplace safe on the plane. That's the fastest way to guarantee they'll make sure it's doubled over with a backpack on top of it in the overhead compartment.
- Be on the plane as fast as you can be, based on what the gate agent will allow. The goal here is to get on the plane and grab an entire overhead compartment to hold everything you and your fiancé are hauling. Don't feel guilty about being a space-hog—you're on your way to your wedding and, between the two of you, you've got enough carry-on luggage and coats to fill a whole section of the overhead storage. If you've been sweet and controlled your frustrated inner diva, you might still luck out with a nice flight attendant offering to store your dress in First Class when you board. Just because the gate agent was a bitch doesn't mean the flight attendants won't be helpful if you're sweet to them. Again, have some

treats handy. I endorse bribery as an appropriate means to an end in the case of your wedding gown.

- Put your bags and everything else across the bottom of the overhead compartment, and then lay your dress over top of the entire thing. It will be scrunched up a little bit, but not nearly as badly as it could be. Make the compartment appear to be full, then shut it. And then watch it. If anybody opens it and looks like they're going to sling their laptop bag on top of it, politely jump up and explain it's your wedding gown. Then give them a cookie and smile sweetly. It sounds so cheesy but I promise, it's worked for more brides than you can imagine. Pray that your flight is not so overloaded that the flight attendants open every compartment to smoosh more things in. Even then, a sweet smile and polite request to "please show mercy for my wedding gown" will get you more help than being aggressive.

- Hang up your dress and take it out of the bag as soon as you get to your accommodations. Most wrinkles will fall out if you're in a humid climate, but you should also have a steamer and iron handy in case you need it. Veils can be tricky. Some fabrics aren't meant to be steamed, so be sure to ask your bridal shop how to fix up your dress when you arrive at your destination so it looks as good as possible when you go down the aisle.

Shipping Your Wedding Gown to Your Destination

Now all my DIYers reading this *must promise me* that you will not ship your wedding gown to your destination unless you are absolutely, positively sure that you have somebody on the other end who knows it's on the way, and will be watching for it. They'll also need to open it up and make sure it arrived in good condition.

Ask your bridal shop to package your wedding gown for shipping after the final fitting. Expect them to argue with you about it because they'll want you to carry it. Remember, you are the client, so ultimately they have to do what you ask. They ship gowns all over the world all the time, and they have the right kind of boxes (your dress probably arrived to them in one of them), and they know how to pack it properly. Let them do it, then mail it with as much insurance as you can afford. Resist the urge to open that box once they've closed it—you'll never get all the tissue paper back in the right places.

Confirm the shipping instructions, address, and timing for delivery with the person who will be accepting your package. Write the words "Wedding Gown" all over the box in a bright-colored marker, along with the telephone number of the final recipient. No, I'm not kidding. The people who deliver packages

It takes a lot of time to steam wrinkles out of a gorgeous gown so that it looks this amazing for your wedding pictures. (Photo by Saul Padua Photography)

are human beings with feelings too, and they will take better care of a wedding dress than any old average package. Insure the box for the maximum insurance the particular carrier allows ($5,000 in the case of US Mail).

Greeting Your Shipments when You Arrive at Your Destination

I will never forget the expression on my fiancé's face when we opened the door to our two-room suite at the hotel where we were to be married. All thirty-two boxes I'd shipped ahead were waiting for us in the not very big suite. The designers of the beautiful Hacienda Tamarindo, one of only three hotels in Puerto Rico to be listed in the book *1,000 Places to Visit Before You Die*, never expected a DIY bride like me to plan the first-ever wedding there that wasn't for a member of the owner's family. We were literally boxed in. The luggage had to go on the bed because we only had a path through the UPS labels.

Fortunately, I had labeled and numbered every box. And there was a list of the contents inside every box (which came in handy when the disastrous mess I was unpacking temporarily hid my clipboard with the master shipping chart I'd created). While I wasn't as organized then as I am now, I was determined to open up everything and make sure nothing had broken. That's your first task too.

Get unpacked first (I wish I had). Then work as a team, and open the boxes in order as much as possible. Depending on how they're stacked, you might need to be a bit more flexible. I remember finding my official "Box #1" behind all the other boxes in the entire room.

Once you've confirmed the contents arrived safely and everything is there, sort the stacks by event, and by what needs to go into welcome baskets or bags, as much as possible. Then go shop for everything else you need at the destination that couldn't be shipped. You literally don't have a moment to lose, and you probably cannot complete those welcome bags for delivery without a trip to the store.

CHAPTER 20

୫୦୦୪

WEDDING PARTY GIFTS AND GIFTS FOR YOUR PARENTS

*A*s a general rule, it is not a good idea to bring your wedding party gifts and the special gifts for your parents with you to your wedding destination. It takes up space, it costs you money to get them there, and it burdens your guests with bringing them back home. Even something as simple as earrings for all of your girls will have to be packed in a carry-on bag, and once they're wrapped up all pretty, that takes up space too. So rethink that plan.

Regardless of where you're getting married, keep in mind that your gifts to the members of your wedding party are supposed to be tokens of appreciation for their participation in your wedding, not what you want them to wear. You can't give your girls the shoes or evening bags you expect them to use for your wedding and consider it a "thank-you" gift. That's called accessorizing your bridesmaids, not thanking them. Same goes for the gentlemen. Even if the neckties you want them to wear are expensive, so you have to buy them or they won't have them, that isn't your "thank-you" present for being in the wedding. It's part of their outfit. The fact that they get to keep it is a bonus for them only if they happen to have the same taste as you—and if they wish to coordinate with the rest of the guys in their crew for all future dress-up events to make sure they won't show up matching each other.

Your gifts to your wedding party, and to your parents, should be thoughtfully selected and given from the heart. They don't have to be expensive if you've been creative; they just need to express your gratitude that they have gone so far to help out with your big day.

DIY brides and grooms may need to spend a little more money to properly thank everyone if the wedding party has been corralled (like it or not) into playing the role of setup and teardown crew at your destination wedding. Yes, I've already advised you to bribe everybody in advance in Chapter 10, but you still have to thank them for their extraordinary efforts after everything is said and done. If you want to do something cute and appropriate after the wedding is all finished, you can treat each of your girlfriends to a manicure (since somebody probably broke a nail working on your décor), and you can send each of the groomsmen whatever tool Sears is gold-plating that year. Yes, they do that, and it's pretty cool.

Wedding Party Gifts for a Destination Wedding

Should what you choose to give your bridesmaids and groomsmen differ from a hometown wedding to a destination wedding? Maybe. It depends on your taste, style, and sense of humor.

I had special Swarovski crystal necklaces made by my friend Kim Guzi for all of my bridesmaids to wear with their dresses on my wedding day, but then I learned that wasn't totally appropriate (thank you Mom, the woman who knows every word of what Emily Post deemed appropriate etiquette circa 1950). I was accessorizing them, not thanking them. So then I went a step further and called a girls' night at my house for all of the crew who lived in the DC area, and brought in a massage therapist for a private spa night. For the out-of-towners, I sent spa gift certificates they could use at someplace fancy in their hometown before or after the wedding.

I also hand-painted champagne flutes for each and every bridesmaid, and wrote them each a very long letter expressing my appreciation and love for them. I shipped the glasses and letters, and carried on the carefully wrapped necklaces in my purse. I gave out the gifts at the bridesmaids' luncheon the day of the wedding.

I'd had a bracelet made for my mother that matched the pretty coral dress she was wearing to my wedding, and my friend Kim had made a bracelet similar to Mom's for me as my wedding gift. Everybody did a lot of boo-hooing at the luncheon, reading the letters

The champagne flutes I gave my bridesmaids at the luncheon on the wedding day.

and opening the gifts. I cried a lot too—maybe not the best timing when you consider I had to look "my best" a few hours later.

Quick DIY confession here—I met jewelry artist Kim while standing in the bead aisle at Michaels, utterly confused. Reluctant to buy anything until I knew what I was doing, I asked her some questions because she looked experienced. We ended up going to Starbucks for coffee, and afterwards I hired her to make the jewelry for me. This is a really good example of hiring somebody to do something time-consuming for you and getting better results than if you'd done it yourself. And in the process, I made a friend I'm still in touch with.

The groomsmen's gifts were harder to choose, but easier to buy. Bill didn't want to give any of the "usual" stuff to his wedding party. When we discussed it (because I had to shop for the gifts), he vetoed cufflinks (because he hates wearing them himself), and he didn't want to do flasks because he figured that anybody who needed it already had one and Bill isn't a big drinker. We settled on personalized grill brands from Williams-Sonoma with each groomsman's initials on them. He'd seen them when we were registering for gifts and it ended up being the first wedding gift we received. Although I wouldn't let him use it before the wedding, he was all excited to play with it, and he figured his besties would feel the same way. Quite a few of our clients have actually given the same gifts to the guys in their wedding parties at my suggestion. Who knew those wedding party gifts could be such a dilemma?

Don't put off shopping for or buying the gifts for your wedding party. How much you spend on them will affect your overall budget, and there's no reason to wait. Do you really want to be arguing about flasks versus grill brands three weeks prior to your wedding? No. Trust me, I did it. It sucks. You can figure out what you want to give your wedding party well in advance and have it ready to either give them ahead of time or bring with you to the destination. If your present is something too unwieldy to bring, consider giving each member of the wedding party a special card with a note telling them what's waiting back home. A bride of mine who gave all of her girlfriends ice cream makers handed out the cards tied to ice cream sandwiches while they were getting their hair done. It was hilarious. Just remember that even if you're willing to ship a big gift to your destination, you're sticking the receiver with the job of finding a way to get it back home with them after your wedding.

Special Gifts for Your Parents at a Destination Wedding

Something small, like a bracelet for your mother or a watch for your father, can be packed and brought with you to the destination. But if you're giving them something more grand that won't fit into your carry-on luggage, plan a dinner together sometime in the month ahead of the wedding so that you can express your appreciation ahead of the chaotic DIY weekend you're all heading into.

Don't forget how much assistance they're giving you—Mom and Dad (likely both sets of your parents) are going to be helping you pull off all the on-the-ground work at your destination wedding. I told you how much my mom had to do on the fly when vendors weren't where they were supposed to be, and how I stuck her and my godmother with finishing all the programs the night before the wedding. Making plans to demonstratively thank them with gifts before they head to your destination isn't a bad idea at all. If you don't live in the same town, it's okay to mail the gifts ahead of time as long as they're accompanied by a long thank-you letter.

Do Something for Your Parents at the Destination

Although all of your guests, including your parental units, will be receiving fun welcome bags upon arrival, you should try to take the gesture a step beyond bags for your parents, if you have the time and resources.

Special floral arrangements waiting in their rooms when they arrive are lovely. Or you can take it a DIY-step beyond that and create welcome baskets with their favorite wine or booze, snacks you know they like, and a few other gourmet goodies. If you know your father likes to munch on cashews in bed at night, get him a big can so he doesn't have to hunt them down when he gets there.

It's not that you have to spend a lot of money on what you put into the extra-special welcome baskets for your parents. You just have to put a lot of thought into it. Each welcome basket should also include another brief thank-you note telling them how much you love them and appreciate their help and support. As I've said before, you're the ones who decided to DIY. Your parents were your unwitting victims. Regardless of how much or how little effort they've put in ahead of the big day, you're going to be keeping them busy now that the actual destination wedding weekend has arrived.

CHAPTER 21

ಹೋಡ

BRING YOUR OWN BRIDAL EMERGENCY BAG—AND I DON'T MEAN THE CUTESY ONE YOU GOT AS A BRIDAL SHOWER GIFT

*Y*ou've read several references to the famous "bridal emergency bag" in this DIY guide, but now you're going to hear all about how to create one that might save the day for you at your destination wedding.

J. Lo was full of shit in *The Wedding Planner* when her emergency kit consisted of a tiny fanny pack with some safety pins in it that didn't show underneath her business suit. That's just not practical. In fact, it's a joke. Our bridal emergency bag at Weddings in Vieques is my husband's former gun range bag from his police department, and I love it because it has a zillion pockets. All filled up, that sucker weighs at least twenty-five pounds. You probably don't need to bring quite so many supplies, but you need to have access to most of it.

Start out by dumping out the cutesy lunch-box "bridal emergency kit" you received as a bridal shower gift and check to see if there's anything in it that's actually helpful. Keep what you can use and repurpose the rest. You don't need to spend the money or space to bring dumb things to your actual destination. This is a fairly comprehensive list of what you need to bring:

- Chalk (white or ivory, depending on the color of your dress)
- Wite-Out (white or ivory, depending on the color of your dress; and yes, they do make it in ivory and it's the best stuff in the world for covering a last-minute "oops" on a gown)
- Shout Wipes
- Q-tips
- Makeup remover
- Bobby pins
- Safety pins
- Diaper pins (if you have a bustle disaster, regular safety pins can't hold the weight of that train, so you have to use heavy-duty diaper pins and cross them over each other under the dress)
- Hairspray (not just for hair anymore; it also gets ballpoint pen out of fabric)
- Eyelash glue (if any of you are planning to wear fakes, because too often the glue in the individual packages you purchased is already halfway dried up)
- Sewing kit (it can be a little one; just make sure it has thread that matches the key outfits in your wedding party)
- Extra thread in appropriate colors for groomsmen's buttons or other wedding party clothing emergencies
- Benadryl (because more than one nervous bride has spontaneously broken out in hives during her wedding day—just be careful how much you drink at your reception if you take an antihistamine)

- Advil, Imodium-AD, Pepto, and any other medication you might personally need on your wedding day
- A new pair of tweezers (this isn't the same pair you're packing for yourself)
- Fabric scissors (because you can't use the funky old kitchen scissors at your venue to trim a thread off your sequined wedding gown)
- A collapsible umbrella (just in case you have a quick rain burst when you're all dressed and ready and headed to the ceremony)
- Hair dryer and hair brush (because Mother Nature isn't always kind, and sometimes members of the bridal party do get wet)
- Deodorant (somebody in your wedding party will have forgotten it)
- Disposable razor (for the bridesmaid who forgot to shave her armpits for your strapless bridesmaid dresses)
- Visine (because most brides do cry on their wedding day, and you don't want to look stoned when you walk down the aisle)
- Nail file and clear polish (you can't fix a mani at the last minute, but you can prevent the problem from getting worse)
- Travel toothbrush and toothpaste kit
- Dental floss (be sure to do a teeth check with the whole wedding party before the pictures begin, because you don't want the dill from those lovely cucumber tea sandwiches at lunch to be evident in your photos)
- Shower cap (you might need it)
- Breath mints
- Lint roller

- Hand steamer and/or portable iron
- Boob tape (useful for a number of things, but mostly hiding gaping cleavage on badly fitting bridesmaid dresses)
- Double-sided tape (good for fixing anything that doesn't have to stick to skin—it loses its sticky quality if you sweat)
- Crazy glue (for loose rhinestones, sequins, and other things)
- Small bottle of clear nail polish remover (because it will take goo off anything)

Be sure to buy new, smallest-size-possible containers of everything. Keep them sealed unless you need them during your wedding weekend. The last thing you want inside your bridal emergency bag is spillage of any form. God forbid the Wite-Out explodes all over everything else. Anything like that should be well contained in ziplock baggies.

You probably have even more things that you've thought about for your own personal emergency bag. If you're wearing stockings, you should bring a backup pair. Or you might need no-skid stick-ons for the bridesmaid's new shoes. If you know your girls aren't responsible, make your own life easier by bringing the things you expect they will forget. Perhaps even a can or two of Red Bull is necessary if you're worried your own energy will be flagging by go-time. A DIY bride has a lot to worry about on her destination wedding weekend, and knowing that her backup emergency kit is in order will greatly reduce stress on the wedding day. Pack what you need. Yes, this is another list you should be keeping as you think of items you need from Day One. The kit should be its own box or bag, although you may ship it inside a larger box. Don't make yourself sort it out when you arrive.

CHAPTER 22

ഇൻൽ

CREATING SPECIAL MEMORIES
FOR JUST YOU AND YOUR FIANCÉ

One of the biggest challenges for the DIY bride and groom is finding a way to make the entire wedding planning process a romantic and fun experience they'll remember fondly. And believe me, you'll have moments where you seriously question your sanity throughout the process.

It's important to celebrate little victories during the planning process. If sorting out (and slimming down) your guest list was a nightmare, it's definitely worth going out to celebrate once those invitations are stuffed, stamped, and in the mail. When the catering contract nearly made you insane and you've finally finished it, go out to dinner someplace you adore and enjoy getting everything you want without having to think about it or negotiate. Finished choosing your bouquets, finally? Go out and buy yourself a bouquet of your favorite posies for the living room of your house. You're working hard planning your wedding and you deserve to thank yourself. If you've spent hours and hours creating custom table runners for your wedding dinner and they all turned

These are excellent examples of easy ways to personalize your dinner tables with your own theme, although painting even zig-zags on burlap takes literally hours. But that's what the DIY process is all about, right?

out perfectly, that's certainly something to get excited about. But don't have dinner on them and risk making a mess and having to start over!

It's also important to remember that your wedding weekend *is supposed to be all about you and the groom.* While many of my brides over the years have definitely belonged to the "it's all about me" school of thought, DIYers tend to lean the other direction. They're more worried about their guests' happiness and enjoyment of the weekend and less likely to concern themselves with their own personal comfort. That's not okay. You have to strike a healthy balance. Remember, these are going to be your wedding memories for the rest of your lives. Just because you've chosen to DIY your wedding doesn't mean that you can't be the "guest of honor" for at least part of it.

Making Special Memories

I strongly urge all brides to go shopping for the *perfect* scent for their wedding day—a new perfume that smells heavenly to them and will always remind them of that day. This scent should be carefully paired with bath gel and body moisturizer that complement but do not overwhelm it. Layered, you'll smell pretty all night long. And this smell is one of the first things that your fiancé will notice about you when you greet him at the end of the aisle.

Do not wear the perfume you've selected before your wedding, no matter what. It's earmarked for the most important day of your life. Wear it to your wedding, and then wear it every single day of your honeymoon. Scents imprint on us, and the smell of that perfume (and bath gel and cream) will make you smile every time you apply it. Smelling it on you will make your husband smile and remember the honeymoon. You should wear it for all your special occasions, and an astute spouse will take note of what you've chosen and replace it when he sees it running low on your dresser. If he's oblivious, dropping a huge hint would be totally appropriate. Especially if there's a special holiday or anniversary coming up.

Create a Favorite Music Playlist

It's entirely possible that wherever you're getting married, there won't be a fabulous radio station to listen to in the car. You may not be able to stream Pandora. And you won't know what's available at your honeymoon destination until you actually go there.

While you're creating playlists of music for your wedding events, or burning CDs for the band to use during their breaks, create your own personal wedding week playlist for you and your fiancé to listen to during the wedding week, on your honeymoon, and for years to come. My husband got all excited when he came upon our wedding week CDs in the music cabinet one day, ten years after we tied the knot. Now that's one of his favorite things to listen to when he's bopping around doing wedding errands for other couples. Every single song on it makes him smile. And we know all the words.

CHAPTER 23

❧❧❧

GUEST MANAGEMENT AT YOUR DESTINATION—WHAT TO DO ONCE THEY ACTUALLY ARRIVE

"The British are coming! The British are coming!" I crack myself up. Maybe that's a little dramatic, but really, you'll feel that way on the day your family and wedding guests descend on whatever destination spot you've chosen for your wedding. No matter how ready you are, no DIY bride and groom will ever feel ready enough. Even if you arrived a week ahead of everybody else, you'll still have that never-ending to-do list to keep on tackling. If at any point in your DIY process you will wish you had actually hired a professional planner, this will be it. But hang in there, you've got this!

Wedding Guests Are Needy Folks

It depends on how well-traveled the vast majority of your guests are, but in general, wedding guests are actually a huge pain in the ass to the bride and groom. Oh yes, you love them and you're glad they're there, but you will feel pulled in one hundred directions from the moment they begin arriving.

The worst ones are the friends who came into town early to make your wedding into their vacation, and they actually think you'll have time to spend with them before everybody else arrives. Not too likely unless they're volunteering to help you stuff welcome bags, right? Set expectations with those friends and let them know that you are thrilled they're arriving early but you can't promise to do anything before the festivities actually begin because, as a DIY couple, you have a lot of T's to cross and I's to dot if your wedding is to run smoothly a few days later. Most good friends will understand. If they don't, put them to work. When they get bored, they'll stop clinging to you. You can meet them at the beach or on the slopes after you've finished your wedding tasks. Don't let anybody distract you into procrastinating, or you'll spend your wedding weekend rushing to get things finished instead of enjoying the fruits of your labor.

Prepare for the Questions

Even if you didn't know your wedding destination very well when you were planning your wedding, by the time the guests arrive, you'll be a pro. That's a good thing, because your destination wedding guests are going to treat you like Julie the Cruise Director on *The Love Boat* Never mind that you answered 75 percent of their questions in your welcome letter (did they bother to read it?); you're the go-to girl and guy for everybody. As DIYers, you have to suck it up and take the responsibility seriously. You cannot ignore your telephone—even numbers you do not recognize—because they could be calling from their date's phone if he's got better reception or a borrowed phone at an airport ticket counter. And they might be calling to tell you they're stuck somewhere and need some guidance.

Know Backup Travel Options Ahead of Time

It seems like once every two or three weddings, there are a few guests who run into travel difficulties (often self-inflicted, because if you miss the first flight in a series of transportation, it is entirely possible you may miss the ferry that was the last leg of your trip, for example). These guests will call you in a panic and ask you what they should do. You have to be prepared with answers.

If you're getting married anywhere in the Caribbean and your guests get stuck someplace overnight because they missed their connecting flight, they're likely going to be spending the night in Puerto Rico. Research the hotel airport, and other places nearby, so you have suggestions for where they can stay overnight for a reasonable price. Give them the number of the hotel, and let them make their own arrangements. Remind them to call their accommodations at your destination, and their rental car company, to advise them of their delayed arrival so they don't find themselves without a room or transportation when they arrive the next day.

Do not offer to take care of all these little details for them. You are not a travel agent; you are the bride and groom, and you are busy DIYing all of your events for the guests who did arrive at the destination on time. If you take on everybody else's travel plans, it's quite possible that you won't have time to take care of yourself and finish DIYing the stuff on your list. Do you really want to look like you made zero effort on your hair and makeup in all those pictures your friends are posting to social media in real time?

When ferries play into the travel plans for most of the group, you should keep a copy of the ferry schedule handy (on your clipboard) and also prepare a list of acceptable accommodations near its port for anybody who misses the last boat. Again, you're not a travel agent; you're a DIY bride. That means it's okay to give the information to your wayward friends and tell them to "do it your-self" when it comes to straightening out their travel messes.

Remind Everybody to Read the Welcome Letter When They Arrive

Sadly, it will be your sharpest friends who totally toss the welcome letter aside as they probe the depths of your carefully constructed welcome bags, especially if they contain booze. I think it's because those same people brought along print-outs of your important wedding information from your wedding website, so they think they know what's going on. But you know how incredibly important it is for them to read the welcome letter in order to know where to be, when to be there, and what they need to bring with them. You spent hours compiling this information and making it easily accessible for them, but now you have to remind them to actually read it when you greet them upon arrival at your destination. Otherwise, you may find yourself short of guests or running late to your own events as you answer calls from confused folks who can't remember where they're headed for your next activity.

Set Behavioral Expectations

No, I'm not suggesting that you sit your guests down and give them a lecture about not drinking until they puke. That would be tacky. But you know who your problem children are in your group, and it's perfectly all right to let everyone know there are some ground rules.

A great example of a time this is necessary is when you've rented a private villa or home for your wedding venue, and some of the wedding party is staying there with you as your guests. The villa could be a $5 million waterfront haven, and it might well send some of your friends over the top thinking they've just arrived at the best Spring Break destination of their lives. While it's true they're going to have fun with the pool and Jacuzzi and outdoor bar and pool table on the deck, it's also important that you make them aware of the need to respect the property. You have a security deposit riding on a bet that you'll be returning that villa in the same condition you got it. Drunk boys throwing deck furniture in the pool late at night is a bad idea. Tossing a zillion cigarette butts all over the yard is a bad idea. On Vieques Island, forgetting to shut the front gates so that wild horses don't wander into the yard and get in your pool and eat your garbage is a bad idea (nope, not joking).

Let your houseguests (because that's basically what they are) know that you have "rented" this house and have a substantial deposit riding on it, so you're asking their help in making sure that everybody respects it and takes care of it while enjoying every bit of it. Also point out that, since they're all invariably part of your DIY setup and cleanup crew, the venue has to be clean and perfect the day of the wedding, so they shouldn't make a mess in the days prior if they don't want to be up at the crack of dawn cleaning on your wedding day. Most villas come with some minimal maid service— they'll freshen beds and replace towels and soap, but they're not coming in to re-clean the entire villa for your wedding because your friends have left a disgusting mess all over the kitchen after making piña coladas at two in the morning. *It's not a hotel* (and I wouldn't recommend making a mess at a hotel that is your wedding venue either). If you approach it like you're all a team, it should be well received. It doesn't mean nobody will try to surf on boogie boards in the pool (and break the boogie board in the process), but it will make most of them think twice about being complete idiots.

"Uncle Charley" and "Aunt Mary"

This is a blog I wrote for Monsters and Critics on April 23, 2015. While it's written from a wedding planner's perspective, I truly believe it says it all, and will give DIYers some perspective on the behavior they can realistically expect from their friends and family during their destination wedding. These people don't become "Uncle Charleys" and "Aunt Marys" overnight, and they don't misbehave at only one event. Who are yours going to be at your DIY wedding?

There is an "Aunt Mary" and an "Uncle Charley" at every single wedding. These are our code names for the problem children that the brides and grooms sometimes (not often enough) warn us about before they arrive. The brother who will be drunk and out of control and the sister-in-law with a mouth that should be duct-taped shut, for example. These are our "special" guests.

For years, our staff has joked about which wedding guests would be our biggest nightmares as each new group arrives. We can usually identify them at the welcome party. If they're not sloshed to the point of babbling incoherency, they're dead sober and latch onto the wedding planning staff like a life raft. Probably because everybody else is avoiding them.

We try to escape, but it's hard. We are paid to be polite. Which is how our "special" guests got their nicknames. "Uncle Charley" and "Aunt Mary" are our gender-specific code words for "watch the heck out for that nightmare guest." And for us, they work. The funniest thing is when it's exactly the people our clients warned us about. Brides and grooms know their guests.

This sounds like a joke, but it's completely serious to us. In fact, even our vendors—from the caterers to the DJ—know about Uncle Charley and Aunt Mary. And believe me, we point them out for the vendors' safety. And if we don't remember to warn them, the bartenders tell us who they are fifteen minutes into the reception.

These people come from all different parts of the wedding group—disturbingly enough, it's too often a member of the immediate family, a member of the wedding party, or their date. The very same people who should be on their best behavior are their own worst enemies, and the bride and groom's least favorite guests.

Here are 10 ways to identify Uncle Charley and Aunt Mary at a wedding:

1. Uncle Charley is the father of the bride who got so wasted during cocktails that when the wedding group got out of control and started breaking things and we asked them to stop (actually, the groom went around and asked them to behave), this Uncle Charley FoB stood up and yelled "bang all you want—we paid for it." Um, actually, you didn't. You rented it. But thanks, now you've bought it. Or rather, your daughter and her new husband will be paying for the damage.

2. Aunt Mary is frequently the mother of the bride or groom who can't handle the fact her ex has brought a date or new spouse to the wedding and drinks too much and tries to cozy up to the male staff. It's embarrassing for the couple (mortifying, actually). When it's my husband, I only let it happen a few times because it's funny to watch him try to dodge Aunt Mary. But if I need to, I'll intervene and ask her to refrain from touching him. We have a sexual harassment policy and it's not just about the female staff . . .

3. Uncle Charley is THAT friend who thinks he's hilarious and is just dying to get his hands on the microphone. This

Uncle Charley gets angry when he doesn't get his way. The brides and grooms leave him off the toasting list for a reason—they don't want to have a wedding roast. And he wasn't asked to sing because it's not a karaoke bar, it's a wedding. And he's awful anyway. As a general rule, he gets nasty and sometimes physically aggressive when he's told no. Not too different from an average two-year-old child.

4. Aunt Mary wishes she were a wedding planner. Usually, we've never even heard of this Aunt Mary prior to her arrival because she's that low on the bride's priority list. And the bride hasn't given her any authority to push the staff around, make demands, or attempt to supervise or control anything. Once rebuffed, she gets pissy and starts drinking heavily. Halfway through the night, she starts heckling the staff. Not even kidding. Oh yes, we take videos of this stuff. Some for personal blooper reels, some for liability purposes. If she tells the bride we were rude to her, I want the bride to be able to see *exactly* how Aunt Mary is spinning the tale of how we refused to create "to-go" containers (a total wedding no-no) and spoke rudely to her. The bride always asks for her own copy of the film because, half the time, Aunt Mary wasn't on *her* guest list. She was a "must-invite" by somebody else.

5. Uncle Charley is frequently a random date of a member of the bridal party who doesn't know anybody at the wedding and tries to latch onto our staff [so he has somebody to talk to] for the evening, including begging us to dance, trying to get us to do shots, and generally making a nuisance of himself. Uncle Charley will spend the entire rehearsal dinner beach party standing next to our staff chain-smoking and telling us stories about his fascinat-

ing life that bore the hell out of us. If it's an Aunt Mary, she'll be hovering around the actual wedding rehearsal (that she's not supposed to attend) offering her opinions on how the ceremony should be choreographed, as if we haven't done this literally hundreds of times.

6. Uncle Charley is usually the party lush. He thinks he's cool because he's getting trashed. We know which table Uncle Charley is seated at as soon as the servers tell us that somebody has just ordered twenty-five shots for one table, in the middle of a dinner service for ninety people. He's already been pointed out to the bartender and his mixed drinks have barely a kiss of alcohol in them because he was wasted before he even got to the wedding ceremony. It's a lot easier to fake his drinks than cut him off—that's the kiss of death at a wedding. Anybody drunk enough to be cut off isn't sober enough to realize that making a stink about it will ruin the bride and groom's night. He's all about what Uncle Charley wants.

7. My husband says that most women between twenty-five and thirty-five who are away from their children for their first vacation become Aunt Marys. Once we had to remove a cousin of the groom from the rehearsal dinner because she was so trashed that she couldn't even sit upright at the dinner table. I was sneaky—she wanted to go outside to smoke and I offered to go with her. A few minutes in, I told her the party had ended and everybody had gone home (she couldn't see into the restaurant from where we were standing) and convinced her to get in my Jeep so I could take her back to her hotel. I took this Aunt Mary all the way into her room, helped her get unzipped, and literally tucked her in, then returned to the rehearsal

dinner and bragged about my accomplishments to the staff. Next day, we find out that Aunt Mary escaped after I left, went to a bar, and invited a random person to the wedding. Of course, we didn't know that 'til some local guy showed up at the venue claiming to have been invited to the wedding by Aunt Mary. That's when we pointed out her 300-pound husband and suggested he get one drink and leave.

8. Uncle Charley is *always* the first one to get naked. This takes place in a variety of forms. Sometimes we walk into the staff room at a villa to get more hand towels during the reception and find Uncle Charley asleep—stark naked—on the bed. More frequently, he takes off his shirt when he gets hot dancing at the reception (super tacky), and then takes off the rest of it to jump in the pool later on. Sometimes he'll keep on his skivvies, but that doesn't leave much to the imagination when he gets out of the water. Ninety-nine percent of the time, Uncle Charley shouldn't be running around naked in front of anyone but his spouse.

9. Aunt Mary often appears to be bipolar. She'll kiss up to the wedding planners (why???) through a couple of events and then suddenly flip on us when something totally unrelated to the staff pisses her off at the wedding or reception, cursing at the service staff or the DJ because he doesn't have her favorite song (which he actually does, but it's on the bride and groom's "do not play" list). God forbid she doesn't like the seat she was assigned at dinner because, obviously, the staff made the seating chart. Not. This Aunt Mary usually apologizes before she leaves at the end of the night. Gee, thanks. Please don't come back to our island to visit. The tribe has spoken.

10. Aunt Mary *loves* to torment the bride. She makes back-handed compliments like "aren't your flowers cute—too bad you didn't do something with orchids since they're more tropical." Or when it's almost show time and the weather is iffy, she'll do her very best to upset the bride under the guise of making her feel better. We recently had a bride who was totally cool and calm despite the fact we were having to implement "Plan B" because of rain. Even the bridesmaids were ready to toss the future mother-in-law down the staircase because she kept going back up to the bridal suite to make snarky remarks about how our team wasn't handling the problem. Everything was under control for moving the ceremony under cover, but she was right, I didn't turn off the rain. Shame on me.

Sometimes a mother of the bride or groom who wasn't allowed to help plan the wedding (for personal reasons of the bride and groom) has to become Aunt Mary to get attention once the wedding weekend arrives. And they usually embarrass their children in the process. There was the groom's mom who requested "We Are Family" at a wedding where not one single member of the bride's family was in attendance. When her son, the groom, accidentally sprayed her in the face with bug repellent when she was bitching about non-existent mosquitoes, I almost wet my pants. You can bet she was a lot nicer to me after I pulled out the first-aid kit and the saline solution.

You've probably attended a wedding in the not-so-distant past—stop and think about who Aunt Mary and Uncle Charley were at that wedding. If you can't come up with anybody, you'd better think a little harder. It might have been you.

It's important that you be aware of the kinds of negativity and bad behavior some of your guests may exhibit at your wedding. Just because you've DIY'd all the centerpieces with love and care doesn't mean that somebody won't say something rude about them. The fact that it's your wedding day doesn't mean Aunt Mary won't get hammered and start belting out show tunes if she gets her hands on the microphone. She does it at every family occasion, doesn't she? Some of these things you'll just have to live with, but if you know something is going to happen that you really would prefer to avoid, consider having a private conversation ahead of the wedding trip with the person who has you concerned. Sometimes gently asking them to tone it down—in the nicest way possible—will accomplish your goal.

CHAPTER 24

 howgh

YOUR EMOTIONAL STATE WILL AFFECT EVERY GUEST ATTENDING YOUR WEDDING, SO PUT ON A HAPPY FACE

*I*t's your party and you can cry if you want to, but if you do, it will ruin your destination wedding for everybody, including your fiancé.

Here's the truth, so absorb it and get over it now: Something will go wrong during your destination wedding weekend. Somebody may cancel at the last second because of a sudden illness. Somebody else might bring a plus-one you were not expecting. If that's the worst thing that happens, you're doing pretty well. Chances are something more dramatic than a headcount problem will occur—whether it's vendor-related or guest-related.

Here's the thing—if the bride and groom handle the hiccups and major dramas that occur in the right way, it won't have any impact whatsoever on the wedding. If you find out that a vendor messed something up and it cannot be fixed, don't tell anybody about the problem and they'll never know about it (unless it's something obvious like the cake not arriving). Keep your personal dramas to yourselves, and try not to be a shoulder to cry on for any of your friends attending your festivities. This is the one time in your life that you don't have to *be there* for everybody emotionally. Your fiancé owns that right exclusively on your wedding weekend. Try to avoid anybody you know will bring you down.

How You React Can Save or Sink the Party

I tell all of our clients to be ready to keep smiling if it starts to rain at an outdoor event. If it's their wedding, we'll have tents or plenty of indoor cover for everybody. But if it's another wedding activity held on a beach or in a park, there might not be a bad weather plan (although it's always a good idea if you can afford to have tents on site); a brief torrential rain shower can be a shocker and cause real stress.

It rained on the beach party Bill and I hosted for our guests at Red Beach on Vieques the day before our wedding. It was perfectly sunny out, the sky was clear, and then out of nowhere it suddenly poured, for less than ten minutes. We could have gotten upset about it and pouted, but instead, my friends and I all headed into the water. Who cares if it's raining when you're standing in the clear blue Caribbean with sangria in your hand, right? All the parents and other guests who didn't do the initial plunge with us came into the water halfway through, bearing fresh beers and sangria refills, and the whole cloudburst turned out to be a lot of fun.

Going off that experience, the first time it rained on one of my clients' beach events, I gave them my "keep smiling" pep talk real quick and sent them into the water. It took a few minutes for the herd to follow them, but when they saw me and my staff standing at the water's edge hurling icy-cold cans of our local Medalla beer at them, they wanted to get in on the act too. Before you knew it, the sun was back out and shining, and every single member of the wedding group was splashing around and laughing.

Jaclyn and Tim could have let the inclement weather destroy their wedding, but instead they had fun with umbrellas while taking their formal wedding pictures outside after we moved their ceremony someplace dry. (Photo by EP Anderson Photography)

That's not the only party it's rained on, but it's a great example of how to keep your "game face" when the going gets tough. You are the de facto wedding planners at your own events, so you are in charge of DIYing your own fun. If you get lemons, make lemonade. And don't forget the sugar. As long as the bride and groom are smiling, everybody at the wedding will smile too (except maybe Aunt Mary, but you were expecting that, since she hasn't smiled since 1992).

On the flip side, I've seen some of the *worst examples* of clients freaking out about a problem with the weather. The most vivid example in my memory came on a weekend when I actually had three weddings (I don't do that anymore or my team will quit and my husband will leave me), and we had two beach parties happening concurrently on the same almost-two-mile-long stretch of beach. They were far enough apart that the groups couldn't see each other, which was probably a very good thing that day.

The weather that weekend was some of the worst I've had in my entire career. I mean horrible, hideous, wet, cold, and awful. It doesn't usually rain in January and although I had "Plan B" ready to go for every instance, I certainly hadn't planned to use them. Unfortunately, I didn't have a choice, and even had to move one couple's wedding to a different venue one day ahead because the rental company called to tell me the winds were too high to make it safe to mount the tent at the other hillside venue. It was really ugly out there.

Bad weather or not, I had about a hundred and fifty wedding guests to keep happy and entertained, not to mention three sets of brides and grooms who were all potential powder kegs. *Nobody wants to see all their hard work and planning go down the drain, literally.* But sometimes Mother Nature goes nuts, and Karma isn't watching, and you have to pull up your big girl panties and soldier on. Two sets of my clients kept smiling all weekend and making jokes about the weather (as they slugged down cocktails loaded with rum), whereas the third set of clients didn't react quite as well.

***

It wasn't raining the morning before two of the weddings when we started their simultaneous beach party setups a few hundred yards apart. It was gray and windy and the radar didn't look good, but the tents were constructed, the caterers were there prepping food, and guests began arriving right on time.

Farthest down the sand at Sarah and Todd's beach party rehearsal dinner, the group turned the rain day into a party. It drizzled, then it poured, then it drizzled, then it poured. All of our staff was wet through to our undies and pretty freaking cold and miserable, although we kept smiling. I'm sure most of the guests were completely blotto—but that was fine, because at least they were all smiling. We kept the music going and they danced under their tent and raced into and out of the water, refilling their cocktail cups. It was one of those days when you're warmer in the water than wet on the beach in the breeze. The bride and groom were laughing (although I knew she was freaking out inside because we'd talked about it) and their positive attitude was pervasive with their entire group of guests. Nobody considered the rainy beach party a washout. Instead, it was a bizarre and funny wedding weekend memory.

Unfortunately, things weren't going so well down the beach at the other welcome party. They had the same setup with tents and music and good food, but the bride was not smiling and the groom was not there yet! I'd popped down the beach shortly after both parties started to check on Sarah and Todd, and returned to the other party expecting to find the same sort of nonsense going on. But it wasn't. Instead, I found a morose bride and a bunch of silent wedding guests standing around under a tent in the pouring rain looking like they were in hell. Yikes!

Apparently, the groom refused to come to the beach in the rain. So I called him and convinced him to come join us.

Ultimately the groom graced us all with his presence, but he'd put a pall over things on that wet and weary day.

How to Handle It if Something Goes Terribly Wrong

You have to be prepared for the worst so that you can be pleasantly surprised when everything actually runs smoothly. But if the shit hits the fan, you have to know what you're going to do to control your emotions in front of your guests.

Dealing with Vendor Problems

Do not tell your guests what's going on if there's a problem they can't see—most of the things that went wrong at my own DIY wedding ten years ago were only noticed by my mother and me because we'd done the planning. Nobody else knew they'd forgotten to serve the coconut crème brulee dessert after dinner—before the cake—so nobody missed it. I was steamed not to see it but kept it to myself (until it was time to settle up with the restaurant the next day). My bouquets were not what I ordered—in fact, they were the complete opposite—but only my bridesmaids knew about the problem because they happened to be standing there when the flowers arrived and I first saw them. We didn't tell anybody else about the mistake that day.

If the problem is something that can be fixed, like no wine glasses on the dinner tables or the DJ playing music that isn't on your playlist, don't overreact about it. If you had a wedding planner, this is something you'd ask her to handle. But you don't, so you or your designated friend who is coordinating all of your vendors that day will have to deal with it and get it fixed.

Regardless of how angry you are, don't let it show on your face. Go find the vendor and ask to speak to them privately, away from their staff and your guests. Don't bring a posse with you (remember, you aren't going to tell anybody else there's a problem). Only the bride and groom, or their designee, should give any instructions to the vendors, good or bad.

Calmly explain the problem to the vendor and ask how they can fix it for you, immediately. It's okay to express urgency, but treat them with the same respect you would want to receive so that you're giving them a chance to fix it. Don't create a situation where the vendor will simply walk out on you or ignore your request. If you come in screaming (even if you're totally right), the vendor will immediately become defensive and any chance at a friendly resolution is screwed.

No matter what, don't tell the guests or your family about the problem unless you absolutely have to, or it's something they've already noticed. If you boo-hoo to your bridesmaids, they're going to get upset too. And if any of them have big mouths and have been drinking, the situation with the vendor could escalate into something very ugly. Try not to tell your parents there's a problem unless they can really help fix it. Your mothers and fathers will be devastated if you're upset, and they will not keep a "game face." Guaranteed.

As good as it feels to know we have all our friends and family behind us when we've been wronged, your wedding day and associated wedding events are not the time to call in your personal support group to prop you up through every hurdle. They're probably having a blast and have no idea that you're upset the pool lights aren't working or that the caterer served margaritas as your signature drink instead of the mojitos you'd so carefully requested. Yeah, you know it's all screwed up, but nobody else does.

Keeping Your "Game Face"

Do your best to correct the problem and then let it go. That's all you can do. You can fight about it with the vendor and try to get some of your money back the next day, but leave that for tomorrow. You're at your wedding. Are you really going to allow the fact that your photographer showed up dressed inappropriately to ruin your night? You can't fix something like that unless you're willing to give up an hour of pictures while they run home to change clothes, so you have to make that lemonade. Express your displeasure at tip time but forget about it for the time being.

Plaster a smile on your face, go get one of those margaritas you didn't order, and get out there and dance with all your friends and family who traveled so far to share your special day. Don't cheat yourself or your newly minted spouse out of having the wedding of a lifetime over missing desserts or unfortunate-looking center-pieces. After it's all over (it takes about a year), you will look back and wonder why you let yourself be so upset about things that weren't that important. Yes, it's important for vendors to bring their A-game to your wedding, of course. But there's pretty much nothing short of the minister failing to show up that should actually *ruin* your wedding.

Keeping a Smile through Wedding Guest Drama

I promise you there will be some drama in your wedding group. You might be lucky enough not to learn about it until you get back from your honeymoon, but in most cases, the drama queens are not thoughtful enough to hide their personal problems from their guests of honor.

What do I mean by drama? It really comes in all forms and you can probably guess how yours will appear just based on what you know about your family and friends, but here are a few of my favorite examples:

- Divorced-parent drama is common. Especially when only one half of the couple has moved on, and he or she is bringing a date. It's not uncommon for the single parent to overdrink to calm their nerves and end up getting very emotional. It's worse when it's the date of the other parent who gets drunk and unruly, because then you have that scene going on, and a crew of the former spouses' friends sitting there taking notes for gossip later.

- If any of the members of your wedding party have had sexual relations with anybody else standing up there with you, expect something to go down at some point during the weekend. There's always somebody who's bitter and will lose it. It's usually a bridesmaid who'll make a poorly executed play for the guy she once did, with his new girl-friend watching, and when she's turned down, she'll fall apart. We've seen a lot of crying bridesmaids at weddings in just this sort of scenario. It's another reason to think very carefully about who you ask to participate in your wedding party.

- Somebody will drink too much and get into a disagreement with their significant other or spouse, or an unfortunate innocent victim who just happens to piss them off. How serious the disagreement is can lead to all sorts of bad things. I've seen a grandfather punch a father, a Mother of the Bride scream at her ex-husband, and once a drunk groom who got into fisticuffs with the bride's stepfather at the after-hours party.

If you see your guests getting into an argument, the bride or groom (or your designee, if appropriate) should intervene. Or have some-one sober and level-headed do it for you. Do not ignore it and let the situation escalate. Weddings are emotionally charged occasions, for some more than others. Nip it in the bud, send them to differ-ent corners to cool off, and let the party continue. If at all possible, get them off the dance floor, away from the crowd, and someplace private where they can get their acts together without an audience stirring them up.

If they don't calm down, ask them to leave. I know it sounds really harsh, but I assure you that your regret at having to ask your friend or sibling to leave will be far less than if you allow the chaos to grow and things to get completely out of hand. The person (or people) who have to be asked to go will be mortified the next day and, hopefully, offer you a heartfelt apology. These are not the sorts of memories you want to have of your wedding.

CHAPTER 25

ଈଔ

DO NOT FORGET TO MAKE CLEANUP, TEARDOWN, AND SHIPPING ARRANGEMENTS FOR THE AFTERMATH OF YOUR WEDDING

Congratulations! You did it! Your DIY destination wedding weekend was a complete and utter success, and you did it all without hiring a wedding planner. You deserve serious kudos. But don't start patting yourself on the back just yet. You're DIYers and you know what that means? What goes up, must come down. All the décor from the previous day's wedding festivities that took hours to hang and string and mount must be taken back down.

All the furniture you moved has to be put back where it was before you moved it (I recommend taking pictures before you change anything so that you can refer back to them when you're exhausted and not thinking clearly the day after the wedding—that's what we do), all of the rentals will have to be stacked someplace for pickup or returned to wherever you got them, the yard has to be policed for cocktail napkins, cups, and cigarette butts, all the trash has to be properly contained (and sometimes removed, depending on your venue contract), and you have to figure out what the hell you're going to do with all the stuff you spent hundreds of dollars shipping to your destination before you take off on your honeymoon. Try not to depart the next day; you're really going to need to be around to supervise teardown and cleanup.

The Teardown and Cleanup Team

The guys who put up your lights and décor are the same friends who will most likely be taking it all back down. It makes sense because they know how they connected it all. But what "makes sense" doesn't always come to fruition if the boys stayed up all night drinking after your wedding and you have to get all the chairs and tables back to the rental company by noon or pay late charges.

Have a plan and discuss it with everybody involved when you talk about how you need their help DIYing your wedding. They'll understand you also need help with cleanup and they'll have the best intentions to help you, but sometimes they just can't seem to get out of bed. Sometimes they're not yet sober enough to be climbing ladders. The bride, who hopefully didn't have to do so much of that the prior day, should plan on being right in the middle of the cleanup.

Getting the groom's dad involved as a sort of team leader can be the best way to marshal your troops—he may have known some of these gentlemen (using that term loosely) since they were kids, and if he tells them to take out the trash, they will. So if he's the one they have to face if they don't show up for your teardown at whatever specified time, they may actually bother to get up rather than suffer his implied wrath.

Make It Fun

You're asking your tired and probably hungover friends and family to help clean up after your party, so you need to make it as fun as possible. Loud music probably isn't a good idea, but having brunch on hand—even something super casual like pastries and muffins—is an excellent motivator. Tell them you'll have breakfast waiting for them when they arrive, and let them get something in their stomachs before the heavy lifting begins.

You can serve mimosas and Bloody Marys to the crew too, but you might want to wait to break out the bar until the ladders are put away. There will be a lot to do, but many hands make light work, as they say. If everybody has assigned tasks and does them, the venue will be put back to rights in just a few short hours. It takes less time to clean up than to set up.

What to Ship and What to Pitch

Just because you spent $100 shipping Christmas lights and Chinese lanterns to your wedding destination doesn't mean you *have to* ship it all back. In fact, you should plan to ditch as much as possible. Do not expect your friends to bring things back for you in their luggage unless you've made arrangements in advance. They've been shopping and added to their own luggage and they don't have room for yours.

True story: Clients of mine bought cases of expensive wine for their after-party and private enjoyment, but they didn't end up drinking half of it. We heard them asking guests to take a bottle as they were leaving the wedding reception that night, and it seemed very nice. Until a guest who did not have a bottle in her hand snarked to us on the way out that she didn't "have enough room to carry back a bottle to return to them in Manhattan." Don't expect your guests to be your Sherpas.

Figure out before you head to your destination what you're going to ship back home after the wedding. That way you can be prepared with the mailing labels pre-printed, permanent markers, and lots and lots of packing tape.

To the best of your ability, limit yourself to keeping only one of each item you DIY'd for your décor unless it's something expensive. You don't need to ship back all sixteen vases you got at the dollar store. You can buy more fake sea glass at the craft store (if you need it) for far less than it costs to ship that weight back. Keep a couple copies of your wedding programs, and one color of each lantern (if they fit in a normal-sized box—otherwise, pitch them). You're going to have to be absolutely brutal in eliminating anything and everything you don't need to keep. It's just not worth the cost of sending it all back when you're spending more on the shipping than it would cost you to replace the items. Don't be sentimental about things you ordered online.

How to Get Rid of the Décor

It's heartbreaking to toss items of value into the trash, so you can try to find a home for them at your destination. If you're at a hotel or a guest house, they'll probably be willing to take whatever you want to leave and repurpose it. If you've rented a private home or used a restaurant as your venue, then you have to be a little bit more creative.

Certainly offer it to the property manager or caretaker; they might be willing to take it and pitch whatever they don't want, taking one thing off your to-do list. On several occasions, we've had DIY brides and grooms we've never met stop into our office and dump boxes of things they couldn't bear to throw out. They figured we could use it all. And we can (some of it, at least).

Don't plan on selling your leftover wedding décor to anybody at your destination because, frankly, unless it's a brand-new stereo system or something high-tech, we're not interested. The local wedding planner doesn't need it, she's got it. The rental company doesn't rent that stuff, or you wouldn't have sent it down in the first place. The property manager definitely isn't going to hand you any cash. Consider it a karma write-off, try to find somebody who will take it and use it, and give it to them for free. Plan this ahead of time because you may not be able to find a landing spot for it if you're tearing down on a Sunday and leaving the destination early Monday morning.

Planning to Ship

Since you've planned ahead and know what you're bringing back, you've held onto boxes and have the packing supplies handy. Put things in boxes as soon as they come down. Start on your wedding night when you pop that guest book, and the leftover favors you're keeping, straight into a box after the reception.

Wrap it all very carefully (because you saved all the bubble wrap from shipping it down to yourself) as you go. If you're leaving on your honeymoon with a different wardrobe the next day, use your dirty laundry to help pad the box. It'll help keep things safe and get your dirty laundry out of your luggage.

You should try to be at your destination long enough to mail your boxes back to yourself when the post office is next open—that's your job as DIYers. You can't dump it all on the wedding planner as you hop on a plane because you don't have one. And it isn't fair to dump it all on your mom like I did. Trust me, I still hear about that. The hotel or guest house isn't going to take responsibility for that unless you give them a hefty chunk of cash up front, and I do mean more than the actual cost of shipping. So

Lili and Alan used a Jenga game for their guest book. Very creative, but important things like your guest book have to be carefully packaged and shipped back.

Lanelle and Brian shipped us a box of rocks for their guest book, and that had to be packaged carefully so the rocks didn't damage anything else they were taking home.

your best bet is to plan to drop it all off yourself at your first opportunity. If you cannot do it for some reason, make arrangements with a friend or family member who will do it for you *in advance* so that they expect to have to take care of that instead of spending the day snorkeling or skiing on their vacation.

CHAPTER 26

ಬಿಂCಜ

WEDDING GIFTS RECEIVED AT DESTINATION WEDDINGS— CARE AND SHIPPING

Smart destination wedding guests do not bring actual boxed wedding gifts to your wedding location. They give them to you before or after the wedding, or have them shipped directly to the address on your wedding registry. With that said, there are always a few wedding guests who aren't that bright, or think the Belgian waffle iron they got you is so incredibly cool that they just had to bring it and give it to you on your wedding day. Not that you would open it at your wedding anyway (super tacky), but you just *had* to have it right then and there. And now it's your problem.

You should have more boxes and packing material leftover than you know what to do with, because you're not shipping back everything you shipped down. Save a few of the sturdier boxes expressly for wedding gifts. You should probably unwrap them to see how fragile they are before packing (a book gets treated differently than crystal wine glasses, for example), but then load them

Beautiful wedding gifts like these hand-painted champagne flutes that were intended for use at the wedding have to be carefully wrapped to arrive back home in one piece after your big day.

up wrapped properly, just like you're doing with everything else you're sending back.

Mark the boxes that contain gifts in some special way so that you open them first and send thank-you notes when you get home. I didn't do that and was mortified when I finally got around to opening the last box, several months after my wedding, and found a wrapped gift inside. I literally hyperventilated because not only did I have no recollection of receiving or packing this gift (because I stuck my mom with that job), but it didn't have a card. All I can do is admit it was truly divine intervention when I unwrapped it to find a Bible—a gift from my godmother who married us—with a message written inside the cover giving us her blessing and wishing us years of love together. Yes, I called her immediately to say thank you and wrote a note the next day.

Cash, Checks, and Gift Certificates

It's becoming more and more common to give monetary gifts, and in some cultures it has always been a tradition to hand the bride and groom an envelope on their wedding night, even if they've also sent you a nice place setting of china back home.

Do not count on receiving cash, though, or you may be sorely disappointed. I've actually had clients tell me that they were planning on "making" X-amount of money at their wedding so they'd have cash for their honeymoon. That's a dangerous way to plan a vacation. Hopefully all the people you think will give you money will do so (I feel tacky just writing that), but you cannot count on making bank at a destination wedding where so many guests spent a fortune to be there with you. They have a year to send the wedding gift, according to official etiquette. You might not get what you're expecting the same day you walk down the aisle.

Handling Cash

If you receive cash wedding gifts, be sure to write down *from whom* and *how much* before you stuff it into your wallet, or you may forget to write an appropriate thank-you note in the midst of the post-wedding chaos that's about to ensue.

Be sure you actually need *that much* cash with you on your honeymoon before you sail away with it, or you might just be risking losing it, having it stolen, or stupidly spending it in a casino when you really meant to put it toward something important. Keep what you think you need and ask one of your parents to take the rest of it home for you. Don't worry, you'll get it back!

What to Do with Checks and Gift Cards

Unless you have no other option, don't take checks or gift certificates on your honeymoon. Give them to one of your parents to take home for you. Sure, you can safely tuck the checks into the back of your wallet, but after a week of fun on your honeymoon, they may not be readable or cashable by the time you get home. Nothing is more embarrassing than having to ask a generous friend or relative to re-write a check. Trust me; I washed one.

Bring a big manila envelope with you in your packing supplies and put all of the cards (with their appropriate contents still enclosed) into the envelope you're sending home. You can write your notes about the cash on the cards they came in and have it all handy in one place when you get back. That way there's no trying to remember who gave you what or risking thanking the wrong person for the wrong gift.

CHAPTER 27

◌◌◌

PLANNING A RECEPTION BACK HOME AFTER YOUR DESTINATION WEDDING— DON'T DO IT RIGHT AWAY

Many destination wedding couples plan a reception of some sort back home. For some it's a casual backyard barbecue; for others, it's the formal black-tie affair their parents wanted them to have in the first place. Whatever you're planning (and trust me, DIYing it at home is much easier than at your true wedding destination, so this one will be cake!), do not schedule it in the same month as your destination wedding. Do it a couple months afterwards and you will never regret your decision to delay.

I really botched this part of my own DIY wedding, but it gave me a lot of insight for helping my own clients plan their at-home wedding events. I've even consulted on the planning of a number of quasi-DIY receptions brides and grooms planned back in their hometowns, and I can tell you that they were all much more relaxed, and had a lot more fun, than I did with my own home-town reception.

We got married on the Saturday of Labor Day weekend in 2004 in Vieques, Puerto Rico, with fifty of our nearest and dearest, and we celebrated our reception *exactly one week later* with a ginormous, three-hundred-person, black-tie affair at the National Press Club in DC. Everything for that was planned and finalized before we left for our destination wedding, and we didn't even get home from our mini-moon until the night before our "second wedding."

We were exhausted, and so were all of our wedding party, family, and friends who had just returned from Puerto Rico too. We were short a few members of our wedding party because we couldn't ask them to come back a week later from Seattle, and they didn't have two weeks of vacation to burn just for our wedding. I sent my gown back with a friend's mom who was leaving the day after the wedding and, miraculously, my dress was perfectly cleaned and repaired (every bustle breaks—I warned you) and waiting for me that morning. But all the fun things I'd planned for everybody—breakfast treats at the nail salon and beauty appointments at Elizabeth Arden—weren't quite as much fun as they should have been, because every single one of us was totally exhausted (and even a little cranky).

Planning Your Hometown Reception the Right Way

Find a date on the calendar at least six to eight weeks after your true wedding date, and clear it with your parents before you start planning. Offer a heads-up to your wedding party too, but don't expect anybody who lives far away to come to both. They might—a few of mine did—but they certainly shouldn't feel obligated. Although you should absolutely, positively send an invitation to every guest who attended your real destination wedding, you shouldn't expect them all to come twice.

Invitations for your reception at home should go into the mail before you depart for your actual wedding if you're having it eight weeks after you return. If you're pushing it later, you can worry about sending them after you've returned from your honeymoon.

All of the DIY wedding tips in this book can be applied to planning your second set of festivities too—it's just going to be a lot easier than it was to plan something thousands of miles away. This time, you can DIY craft to your heart's content because you don't have to worry about how you're going to ship it to the venue. You'll just drop it off the week prior when you're out running errands.

Wearing Your Wedding Gown Twice

I highly recommend wearing your wedding gown to your reception at home if you're having a formal event. Who gets to rock their wedding gown twice? I did it, and it was the coolest feeling. I'd been so careful with it in Vieques that it was lots of fun to go out dancing in it at the clubs in DC with my bridesmaids for the After Hours following the reception.

However, if you're having a casual party where all of your guests will be dressed way down, don't bust out the wedding gown in all its glory. Look for something simple, shorter, and white to wear that is appropriate to the venue and the event so that you don't look ridiculous in the pictures. The groom shouldn't be wearing his wedding suit either if all the men at the party are in golf shirts. They'll feel underdressed and he'll feel stupid. Wear something appropriate and relax. Everybody knows you're the bride and groom. And most of them know you did all of the planning work yourselves. Congratulations!

Many, many times I've said "if only I knew then what I know now" about DIYing my wedding. Having all of the tips and information that I've given you in this book would have made the wedding planning less stressful and the actual execution of the big day a lot more fun for me, and I know it will for you, too. Find someone you can trust to stand in as the boss for you on your wedding day, and as long as you've done everything else I've recommended ahead of time, your wedding should go off without a hitch. Will it be flawless? Maybe not. But if the guests never know that something went wrong, it never actually happened!

Good luck, and happy wedding planning!

This matted map of the wedding destination, meant to be signed by all of the guests, is a beautiful example of a DIY item that doesn't take up much space and truly shows off bride Vanessa's creativity. (Photo by Saul Padua Photography)